Dynamic Living in Desperate Times

Dynamic Living in Desperate Times

A Study in the Book of Jeremiah

CHRIS JACKSON

RESOURCE *Publications* • Eugene, Oregon

DYNAMIC LIVING IN DESPERATE TIMES
A Study in the Book of Jeremiah

Copyright © 2018 Chris Jackson. All rights reserved. Except for brief quotations in critical publications or reviews, no part of this book may be reproduced in any manner without prior written permission from the publisher. Write: Permissions, Wipf and Stock Publishers, 199 W. 8th Ave., Suite 3, Eugene, OR 97401.

Resource Publications
An Imprint of Wipf and Stock Publishers
199 W. 8th Ave., Suite 3
Eugene, OR 97401

www.wipfandstock.com

PAPERBACK ISBN: 978-1-5326-6819-7
HARDCOVER ISBN: 978-1-5326-6820-3
EBOOK ISBN: 978-1-5326-6821-0

Manufactured in the U.S.A.   11/26/18

Unless otherwise noted all Scripture quotations are from the New International Version. All Rights Reserved.

Dedication

To Grace Church of La Verne—for me, a place to belong and become. I love you all!

Contents

Introduction | ix

Chapter 1
Your Potential | 1

Chapter 2
Your Word | 12

Chapter 3
Your Before | 20

Chapter 4
Your Returning | 32

Chapter 5
Prophetic People | 44

Chapter 6
Carrier of Hope Proclaimer of Judgment | 52

Chapter 7
The Ancient Path | 65

Chapter 8
The Dread Champion | 78

Chapter 9
The Potter's House | 90

Chapter 10
Quicksand | 96

Chapter 11
The Fire in Your Bones | 105

Chapter 12
Your Context | 111

Bibliography | 119

Introduction

NEARLY EVERYWHERE WE TURN today, we are met with waves of advertising promoting products and philosophies that promise us a better life. Social media offers a better life through greater levels of human interconnectedness, retail and marketing offer a better life through the options of consumerism, Hollywood offers a better life through the escapism of entertainment and fun, and some Christian prosperity preachers offer a better life through the attainment of more and more blessings from God. Which promise is correct? Where do we turn in these times of cultural stress, political unrest, bloated consumerism, global instability, and anemic spirituality? Do our ongoing cultural and social revolutions contain the keys to a better life, or are the prosperity preachers correct that if we have more faith, God will rain more blessings down on our lives?

This book suggests a different path. *Dynamic Living in Desperate Times* presents some cornerstones that can help us build truly dynamic lives amid the personal, cultural, and spiritual angst of our times. Through a simple study of the Old Testament prophet Jeremiah, we can identify an ancient path that can lead to dynamic living in any generation.

There was nothing easy about Jeremiah's life or times. He lived at the end of Israel's monarchy, and throughout his forty-year ministry, he watched the decline, corrosion, and the eventual collapse of his beloved city, Jerusalem. Yet somehow he managed to live in such stark contrast to the demise of the world around him

Introduction

that author and pastor Eugene Peterson poetically described him as a "towering life terrifically lived."[1]

Hundreds of years after Jeremiah's time, Jesus ministered to the people of Israel amid social and national conditions that were equally grim. Securely controlled under the iron grip of the Roman Empire, the people of Israel ached for a rescuer who would restore their country to its former glory. As Jesus' ministry gained momentum, and speculations about His true identity mounted, He asked His followers what the consensus among the populace was about Him: "Who do people say the Son of Man is?"

They replied, "Some say John the Baptist; others say Elijah; and still others, Jeremiah or one of the prophets."[2] It is interesting that out of all of the guesses about Jesus' identity, the prophet Jeremiah was in the top three. There was something about Jesus of Nazareth that reminded people of the historical figure Jeremiah.

In his book, *The Prophetic Imagination*, biblical interpreter Walter Brueggemann calls for prophetic ministers today after the order of Jeremiah to "evoke a consciousness and perception alternative to the consciousness and perception of the dominant culture around us."[3] Prophets like Jeremiah have always done this. They have always proclaimed a greater reality, more vivid and alive, than the prevailing culture of a given era. Brueggemann pointedly assesses the contemporary American church as "so largely enculturated to the American ethos of consumerism that it has little power to believe or act."[4] Today's followers of Jesus Christ must live differently. We must rediscover our prophetic ethos and embody life in the kingdom of God as it stands in contrast to the dull, passive, consumeristic living of our day.

Despite the desperation in our personal stories and in our world at large today, God has called you and me to dynamic living. It won't look like the fantasy lifestyles promised by our marketers

---

1. Peterson, *Run with the Horses: The Quest For Life At Its Best*, 202.
2. Matthew 16:13–14
3. Brueggemann, *The Prophetic Imagination*, 3.
4. Ibid., 1.

INTRODUCTION

and advertisers or the touted blessings of the health, wealth, and prosperity preachers, it will be vastly superior.

Dynamic lives are not defined by wealth, accomplishments, or notoriety, but rather by an awareness of God's calling and a faithful adherence to that call. In Acts 13:36, the Bible says of King David that before he died he "served God's purpose in his own generation." That is dynamic living—serving God's purpose for us in our own generation—and it is that kind of living that will bless the world and bring life to our souls. Let's eschew the shallow offers from our many advertisers, and let's join Jeremiah on an ancient path where towering, terrific lives can still be built today.

Chapter 1

Your Potential

"'For I know the plans I have for you,' declares the LORD. . ." (Jeremiah 29:11)

DO YOU EVER FEEL like you are living below your potential? Do you ever feel like there is a life that you are *supposed* to be living, but you haven't quite stepped into it yet? Perhaps you are close. If your life were an old school radio maybe you are getting more than silence, maybe you can hear some static or a warbling version of the station you are looking for, but you still haven't been able to fully dial it in.

Do you ever feel like you are *better* than what you are living?

Early in my parenting, I decided that I wanted to be a fun dad. My wife, Jessica, is the quintessential life of the party, and I knew I would have to work hard to keep up with her, so I have always tried to make jokes and laugh with my daughters. Some of my humor attempts have been funny but others have been horrendous. Once, when Madelyn was very small, I made a really terrible joke, and she said to me, "Dad, stop that! You're better than that!"

Do you ever want to tell people, I'm better than this! I'm better than what you think I am. I'm better than my grades. I'm better than my accomplishments. I'm better than my track record. I'm better than the circumstances that currently surround my life. Furthermore, in those moments when you realized that you were better on the inside than what you were projecting or living on the outside, did you ever set out to improve your life and then find it difficult to secure a role model that could show you the way? Sometimes, it is not as easy as one might think to find positive role models today.

Do you remember the Scripture passage in Ephesians 2:20 where Jesus is called the "chief cornerstone"? In the ancient world of construction, a cornerstone could refer to either a ceremonial stone that was placed first as a new foundation was being set, or a literal *corner* stone set in a corner or an arch, that locked walls together and enabled the structure to bear weight. In his *New Testament Commentary*, William Hendriksen observes that cornerstones helped determine the shape and strength of the entire structure and that "all the other stones must adjust themselves to this cornerstone."[1] Essentially, a cornerstone was a model, a blueprint of sorts that helped determine the finished product.

Where are the blueprints for living really great, dynamic *lives* today? Where do we go in today's changing world for examples of terrific living?

In his book, *Run with The Horses*, Peterson remarked, "The puzzle is why so many people live so badly. Not so wickedly, but so inanely. Not so cruelly, but so stupidly. There is little to admire and less to imitate in the people who are prominent in our culture."[2] I know that is a pretty harsh observation from Peterson, but do you ever look at our world today and find yourself agreeing with him? Do you ever ponder our society and wonder, "How can so many people live so far below their potential?" Sometimes, we have to work pretty hard to rise above some of the mediocrity and stupidity that is around us today.

For instance, have you watched any television commercials recently? If you are like me, you rarely watch real-time television programming—you probably stream or pre-record your programs and then watch them later without commercial breaks; however, I

---

1. Hendriksen, *New Testament Commentary: Galatians, Ephesians, Philippians, Colossians, and Philemon*, 143.

2. Peterson, *Run with The Horses*, 14.

recently sat through a thirty-minute program, replete with all of its commercial advertising, and I was appalled. I thought, "How stupid do these advertisers think I am?" The commercials were filled with cartoons of talking dogs and bloated colons seeking relief, and I cringed to think of what one of our great historical figures or a visitor from another culture might conclude about us if they only had access to our television advertising.

Celebrity Worship

We live in a unique moment in history when people are obsessed with fame and celebrity. In personal conversations with Hollywood actors, I have heard that so many people are trying to become famous today that the days of getting "discovered" are pretty much a thing of the past. We used to hear stories about a really beautiful woman walking down the street and getting "discovered." Some producer would see her from afar and run up to her declaring, "You have the perfect face—you *must* be in my next film." Perhaps this kind of discovery still happens from time to time, but with waves of people today desperately trying to break into the exciting world of celebrity and fame, it has become increasingly rare.

Additionally, amid this yearning for celebrity status, we have an interesting phenomenon occurring wherein some people become super famous without doing anything to warrant the fame creating celebrities today whose only claim to fame is that they are famous! We have Facebook, Youtube, and Instagram stars, and some of our most photographed, followed people are not even actors, singers, or artists—they are just *famous*.

Sometimes, in a world like ours with our fame and celebrity obsession, it can be confusing to know where to go to find blueprints for building truly great lives. Where can we go today to find the lives that we want to follow? Are they in Hollywood? Are they in professional sports? Or what about politics or business? Can we look to our politicians for examples of dynamic, high quality living? Are today's business leaders inspiring us to live authentic, admirable lives? If those areas fail to deliver, how about our clergy members? Pastors and church leaders are pretty low on today's totem pole of public opinion. Just twenty years ago pastors ranked near the top of the most respected professional vocations; however, today, fewer than fifty percent of Gallup poll respondents rank clergy members favorably.[3]

So where do we go? If we like being entertained by our favorite celebrities, but we don't actually want to pattern our lives after them, where else can we look? If we love passionately cheering for our favorite sports teams but we have to decry much of their foolish off-court behavior where do we turn? If we are increasingly disillusioned by our political leaders, disappointed by the greed of our business leaders, and suspicious of our spiritual leaders, who is left to help us?

It is not as easy of a question as we might think. This year's Academy Awards presentation will not be giving out Oscars for integrity. After the program, no one will be interviewing "the most faithful spouses of the year." No one is going to create a top ten list of "the ten best lived lives of the past decade." So where do we go to find some human cornerstones?

How about Scripture?

Of course, the Bible might seem like an obvious suggestion for a place to find some quality mentors, and yet sometimes the Scriptures can seem confusing and problematic. A woman approached me after a recent church service to share a struggle that she was having with a section of the Bible. She said, "I just finished reading 1 Samuel, and I am having a really tough time understanding why David is viewed as such an amazing man of God." Then she added, "Maybe it will make more sense when I get to 2 Samuel."

When she said that, I thought, "Oh no. In 2 Samuel, David gets even *worse*. If she doesn't see it in 1 Samuel, she probably won't find it in 2 Samuel either."

---

3. Lydia Saad, "American's Faith in Honesty, Ethics of Police Rebounds," *Gallup News*, December 21, 2015, accessed January 16, 2018, http://news.gallup.com/poll/187874/americans-faith-honesty-ethics-police-rebounds.aspx.

Your Potential

I love King David. He is undoubtedly one of my favorite characters in the Bible. But when you read his life for the first time you can be shocked to discover how deeply flawed his character was. His temper could turn deadly on occasion. He had dozens of wives and concubines, and yet despite all of his available wives, he still committed adultery and then orchestrated a murder to cover it up!

What about Abraham, the father of the nation of Israel? He lied to a powerful foreign king and said that his wife was merely his sister. When the king first saw Abraham's wife, Sarah, he was smitten with her beauty and tried recruiting her for the royal harem, and Abraham obliged. Since Abraham wasn't brave enough to say, "She's with me," he lied and said, essentially, "She's not my wife—you can have her." Fortunately, God intervened on their behalf and chastised the foreign king for his interest in Sarah, and everything turned out okay in the end. However, that event actually happened—Abraham did that—and Sarah his wife had to live with that memory of abandonment and betrayal.

Tragically, Abraham's son, Isaac, ended up doing the exact same thing with his wife, Rebekah. After that, Abraham's grandson, Jacob, grew up and became a liar and a cheater. Moses was a murderer. The Apostle Peter was a blasphemer. Indeed, at Jesus' lowest moment, when He was on trial for His life, His best friend, Peter, swore to a group of strangers that he had no idea who Jesus even was.

When we look closely at the Scriptures we find that the main characters in the Bible are disappointingly non-heroic. There is a popular passage in Hebrews 11—we call it the heroes' hall of faith—and most of the names listed (like Gideon, Samson, and Jephthah) were *not* great lives. We would not want our sons to be like them and we certainly would not want our daughters to marry them.

So, again, where do we go? Are there any biblical bright spots that can serve as human cornerstones for us? The answer of course is, yes! Certainly, there are bright spots in every industry and era, and the Bible highlights one for us in Matthew 16:13-14. When Jesus asked His disciples, "Who do people say the Son of Man is?"

they replied, "Some say John the Baptist; others say Elijah; and still others, Jeremiah or one of the prophets."

Jeremiah. That was an interesting suggestion. Jeremiah was an Old Testament prophet who died more than four hundred years before Jesus came on the scene, and yet there must have been something about his life and character that caused the people to look at Jesus of Nazareth and think of Jeremiah. Some people even thought Jesus was the avatar, the reincarnation, of the Old Testament prophet.

Jeremiah

We might not think about Jeremiah very often in our twenty-first century culture, but the Jewish people of Jesus' day thought about him a lot. He was a powerful figure in their national and religious history, and there was something about Jesus that made people reminisce about Jeremiah. It may have been similar to what our sports commentators do when they compare a new athletic superstar with a similar predecessor. They say things like, "This kid is the new LeBron James or Kobe Bryant!" Or "Wow, it looks like Muhammad Ali has come back to us!"

Most of us might know a few things about Jeremiah. We might know that there is a really big book in the Old Testament that bears his name (Jeremiah, with fifty-two chapters in it, is the longest book in the Bible). We might also know that there are some really incredible passages in the book of Jeremiah such as these:

"Before I formed you in the womb I knew you, before you were born I set you apart; I appointed you as a prophet to the nations." (Jeremiah 1:5)

"'For I know the plans I have for you,' declares the LORD, 'plans to prosper you and not to harm you, plans to give you hope and a future.'" (Jeremiah 29:11)

"The LORD appeared to us in the past, saying: 'I have loved you with an everlasting love; I have drawn you with unfailing kindness. I will build you up again, and you, Virgin Israel, will be rebuilt.'" (Jeremiah 31:3–4)

YOUR POTENTIAL

"This is what the LORD says, He who made the earth, the LORD who formed it and established it—the LORD is His name: 'Call to me and I will answer you and tell you great and unsearchable things you do not know.'" (Jeremiah 33:2-3)

Aren't these incredible promises? All of our Old Testament books contain similar sentiment, but sometimes it is difficult to find it. Often, these passages are buried inside long, descriptive sections about ancient countries and kings, and sometimes in those prophecy books God seems contradictory; sometimes, He sounds like a gentle parent, pleading with His children, and at other times He sounds like a judge, decreeing swift judgment. Consequently, most of us who take our relationship with Scripture seriously have a somewhat complicated relationship with Jeremiah, as well as Isaiah and Ezekiel and the other prophets: we love parts of those books, but we are confused by other parts. We get bored to tears in some sections, but then we are occasionally surprised by a brilliant ray of inspiration, like Jeremiah 29:11 where God says, essentially, "Guess what? I know the plans I have for you—and they are good!"

Through the pages of this book, I would like to extract some inspiration from the book of Jeremiah that we can apply to our own lives today. The book of Jeremiah is actually a book for our times. The details surrounding the state of Israel in Jeremiah's life are eerily prophetic for our times, and amid those desperate, dangerous times, Jeremiah stands as a cornerstone. He is a blueprint that shows us how to live maximized, dynamic lives in the middle of desperate times.

Peterson called Jeremiah "a towering life terrifically lived"[4] and that description touches something deep within the human soul. We were created for towering, terrific living. We yearn to live dynamic lives that tower above the chaos and mediocrity of our modern world. We want to maximize our potential and conclude our lives with such significance that the people who gather at our memorial services will gratefully and tearfully say, "This was a great life—maybe not a famous life or an Instagram celebrity life—but a well-lived life."

---

4. Peterson, *Run with the Horses*, 202.

Dynamic Living in Desperate Times

In the 1998 cinematic *Cinderella* remake, *Ever After*, the narrator concludes the movie with the words, "And while Cinderella and her prince *did* live happily ever after, the point, gentlemen, is that they lived."[5] Jeremiah shows us how to live. He shows us how to live dynamically, discerning and following a calling from God, in the middle of crumbling, controversial times. Whether you are young or old, single or married, a student or a professional or currently unemployed, Jeremiah can show you how to capture a clear vision for a dynamic, towering life. Whether you are happy with today's political and cultural landscape or clinching your teeth in anxiety, Jeremiah can show you how to fulfill God's purpose for you today.

Run with the Horses

Here is one of the big ideas from this study of Jeremiah's life: *dynamic living occurs in the middle of tough times*. Towering lives do not get terrifically lived in the absence of difficulty, but rather in the middle of it. It isn't easy to do. Towering, dynamic living does not happen casually or without struggle. Indeed, Jeremiah struggled so much that history has dubbed him the weeping prophet.[6] He had moments of such outrage and disillusionment that he accused and raged at God, asserting that God had deceived him.[7] He is believed to be the author of the book of Lamentations, a book devoted almost exclusively to weeping and mourning over Jerusalem's capture and exile. It is interesting, though, that despite those low moments God never pulled Jeremiah out of the struggle. He did not let him quit and pursue an easier calling; He actually told Jeremiah to run *faster*.

Listen to Jeremiah's complaint in Jeremiah 12:1–5. He said:

---

5. *Ever After*. Film. Directed by Andy Tennant. Los Angeles: Twentieth Century Fox, 1998.
6. Halley, *Halley's Bible Handbook*, 311.
7. Jeremiah 20:7

You are always righteous, LORD, when I bring a case before you. Yet I would speak with you about your justice: Why does the way of the wicked prosper? Why do all the faithless live at ease? You have planted them and they have taken root; they grow and bear fruit. You are always on their lips but far from their hearts. Yet you know me, LORD; you see me and test my thoughts about you...How long will the land lie parched and the grass in every field be withered? Because those who live in it are wicked, the animals and birds have perished. Moreover, the people are saying, "He will not see what happens to us."

Now listen to God's reply in verse 5. God spoke to the distraught prophet: "If you have raced with men on foot and they have worn you out, how can you compete with horses? If you stumble in safe country, how will you manage in the thickets by the Jordan?"

Seriously? What kind of response is that?

"God, help me, I'm about to faint!"

"Run faster, son."

"God, I'm not joking—I'm sinking here, about to go down for the count."

"I know. And if you can't bear up in these preliminary races, how will you manage in the championship rounds? If you are going under in the shallow end of the pool, how will you swim with me all the way to Catalina Island? Jeremiah, you are falling down in safe country, but what I really want you to do is run with me into the thickets by the Jordan." It is worth observing that the "thickets by the Jordan" were known to be lion country. Jeremiah 49:19 talks about lions "coming up from Jordan's thickets" and Zechariah 11:3 said that the lush thicket of the Jordan was ruined due to the "roar of the lions" therein.

At first, God's response to Jeremiah sounds indifferent to Jeremiah's struggle, but as we continue pondering it we realize that God wasn't being indifferent or unkind. Rather, He was training a champion. He was saying in essence, "Jeremiah, you aren't the first prophet to want to quit. Elijah wanted to quit running even after I helped him outrun Ahab's chariot.[8] Elijah ran with the horses, and, Jeremiah, you will too. There is a faster lane for you to run in, and the life you have always been looking for is hidden there."

I would like to extract three things from this passage and apply them to your life. First, God believes in you. He thinks you can run in whatever place He calls you to. Second, God believes in *Himself*. If you do fall down in the race, He is convinced that He can get you up and running again. One of my mother-in-law's favorite inspirational quotes says, "I steadier step when I recall that if I slip, thou dost not fall." Third, there is a faster lane for you to run in. If you are tired today, if you are sick of running, or if you want to quit, I am so sorry and I empathize. However, you have to keep on running. God does not have a white surrender flag for you to run up the flagpole. Rather, He has a message for you: "Change to a faster heat. Slide over to a faster lane. There is more for you!"

God's question to Jeremiah hangs in the atmosphere throughout every generation, waiting for someone to answer it: "What is it you really want? To shuffle along with the crowd, or run with the horses? Do you want to live a forgettable life or a towering one, a flimsy life or a dynamic one?"

There are two ways that we can define humanity: minimally or maximally. Minimally, we are nothing more than "featherless bipeds."[9] That's how Plato described a human, and from a minimalist perspective it is true. However, maximally speaking, it is a different story. The Scriptures say that we are "a little lower than God."[10] So, do you want to live minimally or maximally? And please note that if you are so exhausted by life that you really don't care about maximal living, it doesn't get much easier when we settle for a slower heat. Jeremiah was losing in his race against *footmen*. He couldn't even keep up when he was living minimally. In fact, it might even be more difficult for us to live minimally than maximally because something dies in the human soul when

---

8. See 1 Kings 18:46

9. Desmond, *Being and the Between: Political Theory in the American Academy*, 106.

10. Psalm 8:5 NASB

Your Potential

we sell out or settle for second best. We are going to be tired either way, so we may as well step up and go for it. We may as well live maximally and dynamically, trusting God to sustain us along the way. We may as well step up and run with the horses and see where the race eventually takes us.

Dynamic lives:

1. Run in a faster heat.

Questions for Discussion

- Where do you typically turn when you are looking for a role model to show you the way?
- Who are some of your most significant role models (living or deceased)?
- When Jeremiah was already fainting from exhaustion, why would God tell him to step up and run faster?
- Despite Jeremiah's internal and external challenges, God called him to run with the horses—where do you sense God calling *you* to run faster?
- What would it look like for you to live "maximally" rather than "minimally"?

CHAPTER 2

Your Word

"The word of the LORD came to me saying. . ." (Jeremiah 1:4)

EDGAR ALLAN POE ONCE remarked that a book is not worth reading if it does not grip the reader from the opening sentence. Unfortunately, Jeremiah lived too soon to hear Poe's advice. At first glance, the book of Jeremiah is anything but gripping. It begins with Jeremiah's authorial introduction and then a short list of Israeli kings punctuated by a brief historical notation:

> The words of Jeremiah son of Hilkiah, one of the priests at Anathoth in the territory of Benjamin. The word of the LORD came to him in the thirteenth year of the reign of Josiah son of Amon king of Judah, and through the reign of Jehoiakim son of Josiah king of Judah, down to the fifth month of the eleventh year of Zedekiah son of Josiah king of Judah, when the people of Jerusalem went into exile. (Jeremiah 1:1–3)

This is a very tedious introduction, not nearly as exciting as Poe's opening lines in "The Raven" or "The Fall of the House of Usher." Even if we care about Jeremiah's hometown or we have an interest in the genealogies of Israel's final kings, these opening verses certainly don't grip us by the collar and make us desperate to read more. We don't skim these opening sentences and exclaim,

Your Word

"Oh my God—Hilkiah and Anathoth and Zedekiah! What comes next? I can't put this down! I think I'll read the whole book in one sitting." When we get to Jeremiah, most of us don't know—or care—where "Anathoth in the territory of Benjamin" is and most of us are a bit fuzzy when it comes to Israel's succession of kings.

We think, "Who was Josiah again? He was one of the good kings, right? Who was Amon? Who were Jehoiakim and Zedekiah again? Oh wait, the exile. I know that one! That's when they were conquered by King Nebuchadnezzar and carried into captivity in Babylon, right? That's when Jerusalem was conquered, broken, and burned, and Daniel and his three friends were captured."

However, there is actually something powerful being communicated in the opening words of Jeremiah's book, and if we can dip just a little bit below the surface, we might indeed find that this introduction does grip us and inspire us to read on. Jeremiah's introduction highlights a simple but powerful truth: *God communicates with His people and He never stops communicating.*

Jeremiah's opening words tell us that the word of the Lord came to Jeremiah when he was a very young man, during the reign of the good king Josiah. Josiah was possibly the best king that Israel ever had, as 2 Chronicles 34:1–3 explains:

> Josiah was eight years old when he became king, and he reigned in Jerusalem thirty-one years. He did what was right in the eyes of the LORD and followed the ways of his father David, not turning aside to the right or to the left. In the eighth year of his reign, while he was still young, he began to seek the God of his father David. In his twelfth year he began to purge Judah and Jerusalem of high places, Asherah poles and idols.

That is remarkable! At sixteen, Josiah began to personally seek God, and at twenty, he launched a campaign to reform the country and bring Israel back to God. It was in the first year of that campaign that "the word of the LORD came to Jeremiah" for the first time.

The opening text goes on to say that the word of the Lord also came to Jeremiah during the reigns of Jehoiakim and Zedekiah,

Dynamic Living in Desperate Times

"when the people of Jerusalem went into exile" (Jeremiah 1:2–3). Unfortunately, those final words are tragic ones, because even though Josiah was an amazing king who initiated some remarkable religious reforms, the country was too far gone by the time he ascended the throne. It had already crested the top of the proverbial waterfall and even though Josiah slowed its decline and destruction, it was too late. It was on a fast track for disintegration, and that is when King Jehoiakim came on the scene. Where Josiah was the inspired beginning of Jeremiah's story, Jehoiakim was the villain of the story. Jehoiakim hated Jeremiah. He constantly resisted Jeremiah's teachings and prophecies, and he ultimately led Israel to the brink of ruin. He had the dubious distinction of overseeing the ultimate collapse of the nation.

King Zedekiah—the final king listed in the introduction to the book of Jeremiah—was not evil like Jehoiakim; he was simply weak and wishy-washy, which can sometimes be almost as frustrating. He liked Jeremiah, and he often summoned him to ask for his counsel, but he seldom ever did what Jeremiah said. This was partly due to Jeremiah's lack of popularity—Jeremiah was always a lone voice speaking out against the current tide of the culture (towering, dynamic lives are seldom popular or glamorous), and Zedekiah usually preferred going along with the popular majority.

Ultimately, Israel was broken, conquered by Babylon, and swept into a seventy-year exile, followed by several centuries of desolation and oppression; however, please notice the common denominator in Jeremiah's story throughout the accounts of those various kings. From the good king Josiah to the villainous king Jehoiakim to the weak king Zedekiah, *the word of the Lord kept visiting Jeremiah.* "The word of the LORD came to him in the thirteenth year of the reign of Josiah...and through the reign of Jehoiakim...down to the fifth month of the eleventh year of Zedekiah...when the people of Jerusalem went into exile" (Jeremiah 1:2–3).

For forty years, from Jeremiah's initial calling in his youth to the collapse of the nation of Israel, the word of the Lord came to Jeremiah. God used a word to launch Jeremiah's ministry at the beginning, and then at the end of the story when everything was collapsing around Jeremiah, God was still speaking to him. As Brueggemann has stated, God is "not the majestic, unmoved Lord but rather the one with the passion who knows and shares in the anguish of the brother and sister."[1] God never fails to speak to His people.

Throughout all of the highs and lows of spiritual renewal and decline, God spoke to Israel. Even when they refused to listen to Him and were overcome and swept into captivity, God continued reaching out to them through His prophets. When the nation went into exile, God raised up prophets like Ezekiel, and He immediately began speaking to them again. Here is truth: God will never stop reaching out to His loved ones; He will never stop reaching out to *you*. Even when it appears that you or the people you love have failed too badly or have drifted too far from Him, God's word never stops chasing you. You have not been left alone; you and your loved ones are being pursued, tracked down by the word of the Lord. Dynamic living begins when we hear and respond to that word.

Do You Have a Word Yet?

At this point in your personal story are you able to identify a guiding word that God has spoken over your life? Are you confident that you have truly heard from the Lord? Consider this sentiment from Dallas Willard. He wrote: "Hearing God? A daring idea, some would say—presumptuous and even dangerous. But what if we were made for it? What if the human system simply will not function properly without it?"[2] He continues, "Isn't it more presumptuous and dangerous, in fact, to undertake human existence *without* hearing God?"[3]

---

1. Brueggemann, *The Prophetic Imagination*, 92.
2. Willard, *Hearing God: Developing a Conversational Relationship with God*, 11.
3. Ibid., 11.

Dynamic Living in Desperate Times

God has a word for our human existence, and any of us who would live dynamically must discover what that word is. Jesus stated that, "Man shall not live on bread alone, but on every word that comes from the mouth of God" (Matthew 4:4). Truly dynamic, towering lives are not exclusively human; they possess a touch of the divine in them. They carry the life and freshness of a word from God, and they embody a beautiful, and sometimes messy, blend of both the earthly and the divine.

I hope you are chasing more than your own human dreams for your life. I hope you are not just following man's best wisdom or advice for living, rather, I hope you have touched something transcendent and divine. Although we human beings are remarkable creatures with staggering ability to discover, create, and design, we were made for more than what we can accomplish through our own efforts. Dynamic lives stand tall amid shaky times when they receive and respond to a word from God, working that word into the very essence of their nature and identity.

The opening words of Jeremiah's book express this blending of the human and the divine: the words in his book were God's words but they were Jeremiah's words too. Jeremiah was doing the talking but God was the one who was actually speaking. "The words of Jeremiah son of Hilkiah...the word of the LORD came to him" (Jeremiah 1:1-2).

This is true of the Bible in general. It is a human book, written, assembled, and prepared by humans, but it is also divine. The human authors did not go into trances and lose their personalities when they received their revelations from God. Nor did the Bible drop down out of heaven pre-written and prepared. God used humans, like Moses, David, and Baruch (Jeremiah's assistant), to shape it and give it context, and each of their unique personalities is expressed amid its divine content. Dynamic lives embody a merger between the human and the divine, as human beings receive and respond to a word from God.

The Three Lights of Divine Guidance

If you need encouragement regarding your ability to receive a word from God, consider a simple thought and starting point from F.B. Meyer, a famous London pastor in the nineteenth century. Meyer was instrumental in introducing much of the English-speaking world to an understanding of the deeper life of Christ and the ability to perceive His personal guidance, and in his classic book, *The Secret of Guidance*, he wrote about the three lights of divine guidance: the inner prompting of the Holy Spirit, God's word as revealed in the Bible, and the confirmation of outside circumstances and events. He wrote, "God's impressions within and His Word without are always corroborated by His providence around, and we should quietly wait until these three focus into one point."[4] He continued:

> Sometimes (we) sigh for an angel to come to point the way (but) the time has not come for (us) to move. If you do not know what you ought to do, stand still until you do. And when the time comes for action, circumstances, like glowworms, will sparkle along your path. You will become so sure that you are right, when God's three witnesses concur, that you could not be surer though an angel beckoned you on.[5]

When these three lights converge, when the still, small voice of the Holy Spirit within us converges with Scriptural truth and outside confirmations, our confidence and peace will radically increase. Meyer observed, "So much of our power and peace consist in knowing where God would have us be and in just being there."[6]

A Fourth Light: Your Community

Ultimately, the word of the Lord to us will also be confirmed by others. Granted, there may be times in our lives when we must

---

4. FMeyer, *The Secret of Guidance*, 28.
5. Ibid., 29.
6. Ibid., 19.

obey God's leading, even if other people think we are wrong; however, as a rule, God's work and calling in our lives will be confirmed by our community. When the apostles wrote some instructions to the Gentile believers in Acts 15:28 they said, "It seemed good to the Holy Spirit and to *us* (emphasis added)." They did not say, "It seemed good to the Holy Spirit and to James or Peter or John." God's word was confirmed by His *people*.

Additionally, when Paul and Barnabas were sent out from Antioch to preach to the known world, their commissioning occurred in a communal context as well. Acts 13:1–2 tells us, "Now in the church at Antioch there were prophets and teachers...while they were worshipping the Lord and fasting, the Holy Spirit said, 'Set apart for me Barnabas and Saul for the work to which I have called them.'" God most definitely speaks to us individually, but His word in our lives will also be attested to and confirmed by our community.

God has a word for us, regardless of who happens to be sitting on the throne in a given moment in time. Whether the good king Josiah is on the throne or whether villains are in control, dynamic lives persist in seeking God's voice and responding to what He says. As they do, they discover the powerful truth that with God hope is never lost, not even when Jerusalem falls and Babylon wins the day.

Several centuries after King Zedekiah oversaw the destruction of Jerusalem, Jesus Christ began His ministry, and He asked His followers what people were saying about Him. He asked, "Who do people say the Son of Man is" (Matthew 16:13)?

They replied, "Some say John the Baptist; others say Elijah; and still others, Jeremiah or one of the prophets" (Matthew 16:14).

Why would they think that? Why would some people conclude that the miracle-working carpenter from Nazareth was the reincarnation of the prophet Jeremiah? Because Jeremiah's story was a history of the unfailing word of God to His people, and in Jesus, God was speaking again.

So, what is *your* word? What has God spoken to you throughout the different seasons of your life? What did He say to you when you were young and things were good? What did He say during the desert seasons you have experienced? What is He saying now, about your family, about your future, about *you*? What has your community helped you discern?

If your initial, visceral response is, "I have no idea. I have no clue. I don't know if God has ever spoken to me," please slow down, lean in, and listen. God does have a word for you, and if you want it, He will enable you to hear it. Dynamic living occurs as we hear God's message and move in greater sync with what He is saying.

Dynamic lives:

1. Run in a faster heat.
2. Are fueled and sustained by a word from God.

Questions for Discussion

- How confident are you in your ability to hear from God?
- Do you have a life word—a big picture, guiding word from God for your life?
- Is it easy or difficult for you to sense the still, small voice of the Holy Spirit within you?
- Of F.B. Meyer's "three lights of divine guidance," which of the three is the most challenging for you to perceive?

CHAPTER 3

Your Before

"Before I formed you in the womb I knew you, before you were born I set you apart; I appointed you. . ." (Jeremiah 1:5)

"BEFORE I FORMED YOU in the womb I knew you, before you were born I set you apart; I appointed you as a prophet to the nations." Aren't those powerful, hope-filled words? Don't they stir an ache in your soul and bring a tear to your eye? They speak of legacy, purpose, and destiny, and they promise a better day. And, incidentally, they are not just true of Jeremiah; they are also true of *you*. Before *you* were formed in the womb, God knew you. Before you were born, you were set apart. You were appointed to something—maybe not as a prophet like Jeremiah was, but as something.

The word "before" is very powerful. Have you noticed that it is almost impossible to understand what is happening "now" unless you understand what happened "before"? Before informs now.

"Why are they so guarded and self-protective?"

"Well, before you met them they got really hurt in some relationships. Nobody defended them, so they feel like they need to defend themselves."

"Why is Grandpa so quiet? Why won't he ever talk about himself?"

Your Before

"Well, *before* he was your grandpa he saw some things in the war that no one should ever have to see—and those things still affect him today."

We can almost never judge what is happening *now* until we know what came *before*. In *Epic: The Story God is Telling*, author John Eldredge illustrates:

> You come home one night to find that your car has been totaled. Now, all you know is that you loaned it for a couple of hours to a friend or your teenage daughter, and now here it is, all smashed up. Isn't the first thing out of your mouth, "What *happened?*" In other words, "Tell me the story." Somebody has some explaining to do, and that can be done only in hearing the tale *they* have to tell. Careful now—you might jump to the wrong conclusion. Doesn't it make a difference to know that she wasn't speeding, that in fact the other car ran a red light? It changes the way you feel about the whole thing. Thank God, she's all right.[1]

Before gives now context. Thus, biographers dig through family archives and psychologists try to sift through childhood memories; the before is the root system of the now.

The opening verses in Jeremiah's story give us insight into some things that happened before you ever came on the scene, and I am not simply referring to the joining of a sperm and an egg. Yes, that happened before you were born, but that moment—that act—does not reach back far enough.

It might be true of a person's story that, "My parents wanted me and planned for me and couldn't wait for me to be born."

Or someone else might say, "I was an accident. My parents thought they were done with kids and then, Oops . . . I happened."

Others might say, "I never knew my father. I was the product of a one-night stand."

Or, "I was adopted."

Or, "Yes, I was wanted, but there were fertility issues so I came from an egg or a sperm donor."

---

1. Eldredge, *Epic: The Story God is Telling*, 3.

All of those scenarios might be true for people, but none of those scenarios goes back far enough. Each gives only some of the *conjugal* details of how a person was conceived. None really tells us what was happening *before*. Before your mom and dad hooked up, you already existed in the mind of God. You were already wanted. You already mattered. By not going back all the way to God we limit ourselves to a shrunken "before" and that can hurt us.

It is a wonderful thing to have been wanted by our natural parents. It is a tremendous gift to discover that our mom and dad were excited by the prospect of our birth. I am extremely fortunate because I have actually read love letters that my mom and dad wrote to each other when my mom was pregnant with me. They were so excited to have me that they could hardly wait to meet me. They viewed my birth as an expression of the depths of their love for each other, and they were calling me nicknames before I was even born. It is an amazing gift for someone to know that they were wanted like that. Yet what if that was not your story? What if your parents *were not* excited to have you? What if they were not planning on getting pregnant and your conception filled them with grief and anxiety? What if they considered aborting you? What if *that* was your before? Some people spend their entire lives feeling unloved and unwanted because their "before" only goes back as far as the night their mom and dad had sex.

Before Your Before

Jeremiah would shout to us, "Oh, but there is more! Before you started forming in the womb, *God* knew you. *God* wanted you. It may have been an accidental situation, or even a painful one, that brought you into the world, but that is not your origin. God is." And if you are tempted to think, "Well, this passage is about Jeremiah, how do I know that I can apply it to my situation?" please consider a couple of things. First, all throughout Scripture God is clearly seen as the author of life. We humans, made in God's image, do indeed have life-producing power that we get to steward and manage, and yet, just because I, or a fertility doctor, decides to make a union with a sperm and an egg, it does not mean that we are the authors of life. We are not. God is.

Second, the Bible also states that God is no "respecter" of persons (Acts 10:34), and this means that He did not love Jeremiah more than He loves you. If you are the parent of multiple children, you certainly understand that your love can be different and unique from child to child, but you seldom have a hierarchy; you deeply love all of your kids. And so it is with God. He spoke to Jeremiah about a powerful "before" but that word was also true of other people, like King David. In Psalm 139:13-16 David exclaimed:

> For you created my inmost being; you knit me together in my mother's womb. I praise you because I am fearfully and wonderfully made; your works are wonderful, I know that full well. My frame was not hidden from you when I was made in the secret place, when I was woven together in the depths of the earth. Your eyes saw my unformed body; all the days ordained for me were written in your book before one of them came to be.

Those words were true of Jeremiah and David, and they are also true of *you*.

Additionally, God is the only "before" that actually makes sense. If you and I are nothing more than our chemistry and biology, why do we ache so much to be loved and significant and *known*? If we are nothing more than the natural product of a simple, sexual hookup, why do we dream of eternal things like relationship and destiny and heaven? Why do we care so much whether we are loved or whether our life counts? Those are more than evolutionary urges. If we only exist to perpetuate our species, then it makes sense that we would go into heat and want to have sex, but why would we be gripped with so much existential angst about our identity?

The Bible says that God, not your mom and dad, is your before, and it also says that He has placed eternity inside your soul. Ecclesiastes 3:11 says, "He has made everything beautiful in its time. He has also set eternity in the human heart." This explains why you will never be fully satisfied by temporal things like a good job, lots of money, or six-pack abs. Those are not the essential elements that towering lives are made of, and you are so much bigger than all of that. There is so much that came before you for you to ever be content with little things like that.

Known

"Before I formed you in the womb I knew you" (Jeremiah 1:5).

Before you were formed you were "known." That's amazing. The word "knew" is the Hebrew word *yada*. *Yada* is one of the most powerful words in the Bible for knowing something. There are multiple levels of knowing something. Someone can know enough about World War II history to win a round in *Jeopardy*, but that is not the same thing as being a World War II *historian*. Additionally, being a World War II historian is not the same thing as being a World War II *veteran*. *Yada* means to know completely and experientially.[2] This means that you were fully known, and God still wanted you. You were not rejected.

One of our great human fears is being truly known. Although we long to be known, it can also be a terrifying prospect. We fear, if you really knew me you wouldn't love me. However, when we begin to understand our "before" we start realizing that those fears have already been dealt with—God knew us completely and He still wanted us. "Before I formed you in the womb I knew you, before you were born I set you apart; I appointed you as a prophet to the nations." (Jeremiah 1:5).

It is interesting to note that *God knew Jeremiah before Jeremiah knew God*. All of this "before" was happening before Jeremiah had any active role in it. That is huge. God does not accept us because we ask Him to, or because we are good Christians or good people. Before we were good at anything, He saw us and loved us and allowed us to exist. *We are known before we know.* Understanding this can change how we approach our lives. We are not striving to

---

2. Zodhiates, *The Complete Word Study Old Testament*, 1806, 2321.

be loved; we are loved. We do not have to rush around trying to figure everything out because we can go to the one who already knows. We do not live our life like it is a puzzle to be solved; we relate with the one who has already assembled the puzzle and knows the end from the beginning.

The human story did not begin with us. We were born into a story that was already in motion. God initiated it before we came on the scene, and God Himself will eventually conclude it. Our part is to respond to Him and partner with Him, and when we do that we begin to land on the purpose for our existence. Jeremiah came into the world prepackaged with a purpose to fulfill, and he began discovering that purpose when a word from God came to him during the thirteenth year of King Josiah's reign. When I was in college, I wrote a short poem about discovering purpose.

> There's a desperate quest of which all men seek,
> Yet of its nature few will speak.
> They ask the same question, "Who is *me*?"
> All men are searching for their identity.
> They look for themselves in gems and in sword,
> I found myself in the hand of the Lord.

In Isaiah, God expresses this sentiment when He says, "I have written your name on the palms of my hand" (Isaiah 49:16, NLT). Consider that. God tattooed your name, your identity, on the palm of His hand! So when God extends what the Bible calls "the right hand of fellowship" to you, you begin discovering who you really are.[3] Colossians 2:10 says, "In Christ you have been brought to fullness." The word "fullness" is a fascinating word in the Greek language that means to fill a net with fish or a house with a sweet perfume.[4] What is the purpose of a fishing net? To catch fish! What is the purpose of a home? To house a fragrant atmosphere of love, life, safety, and relationship.

Colossians 2:10 is telling us that when we walk with Jesus we connect to our before, and our lives start inflating with purpose.

3. See Galatians 2:9
4. Zodhiates, *The Complete Word Study New Testament*, 662, 948.

What is *your* purpose? Maybe it is to be a prophet. Maybe it is to be a mom. Maybe it's to be a missionary, or an interior decorator.

A few years ago, our church staff moved into new administrative offices and I asked my daughter, Madelyn, to help me decorate my new space. Ever since she was a little girl, Maddie has had an eye and a passion for design and décor. As a child, she would beg us to buy her new throw pillows or to replace an existing lampshade for a trendier one, so I asked her to help me arrange my furniture and position my books and pictures and plaques. Naturally, she did a beautiful job, and as we were driving away she remarked, "I feel so happy inside." Her comment prompted a great conversation between us about the joy that fills us when we exercise our gifts and live inside our purpose; it is kind of like what happens when your fishing net comes up full.

Who Were You When You Were Young?

The word about his purpose came to Jeremiah when he was *young*. In Jeremiah 1:6, he replied to God's comments about his "before" by saying, "Alas, Sovereign LORD, I do not know how to speak; I am too young."

Who were *you* when you were young, before peer pressure, rejection, and insecurity started twisting you up inside? When we are young, we naturally express certain aspects of our purpose. If you had spent time with the childhood me, before I got too damaged by sin, ego, and human failures, you would have seen little glimpses of what God wanted to do with my life. Sometimes the journey of our adulthood is the recovery of our childhood, and the older we get and the more healed we become the more the childhood version of our true self gets restored.

The Bible does not tell us exactly how old Jeremiah was when God initially spoke to him, but scholars guess that he was perhaps a year or two younger than King Josiah, possibly late teens or twenty years old.[5] It is worth remembering who we were dur-

---

5. Halley, *Halley's Bible Handbook*, 309.

ing our youth and young adulthood years to see if there were any indicators of God's larger purpose for our lives. It makes sense that therapists and psychologists often ask: "What was your childhood like? What were you like as a kid?" Our childhoods contained more than the seeds of our adult dysfunction; they also contained snapshots of our purpose.

Appointed

As Jeremiah moved deeper into his purpose, he learned that God had *appointed* him to something. That word shows up twice. In verse 5 God said, "I have appointed you as a prophet to the nations" and in verse 10 He added, "See, today I appoint you over nations and kingdoms." The word "appoint" is the Hebrew word "Nathan" and the word "Nathan" means "to give."[6] In popular baby name books the name Nathan is defined as meaning "a gift from God."

So here is what happened. Before your mom and dad hooked up, God had an incredible idea: you. He thought, "Wow, if I form things just right, and if I breathe my nature into this child, and if I set them apart for a specific purpose, I can fashion them in such a way that they become a gift for the world." God created you to know you, to love you, *and to give you away* for the needs of the world. This is why self-centered living is the most unsatisfying way to live. In the short term it can be fun to live a shallow, pleasure-oriented, self-consumed existence, but that kind of living eventually leaves a person bankrupt inside because we were not created to live only for ourselves, rather, we were created to be a gift for someone else.

The name Jeremiah has two possible meanings. Sometimes, translators interpret it as the Lord exalts, or sometimes as the Lord hurls or throws.[7] Both definitions work. God did, indeed, lift Jeremiah up to hurl him like a javelin to the nations, and when

---

6. Zodhiates, *The Complete Word Study Old Testament*, 835, 2,560.
7. Ibid., 1,806, 2,529, 2,586.

Jeremiah lived his purpose and spoke his prophetic words to the nations he became a gift for those people. He helped them uproot and tear down things that shouldn't be there and then plant and build up some things that should.[8]

Have you discovered yet who you are supposed to be a gift for?

Special Needs Children

I would like to make a quick comment here about special needs children. When we discuss God's formation of humans in the womb and His setting them apart from birth for their purpose it raises some questions: "What about special needs children? What about people who are born with diseases or disabilities? Is that God's plan and purpose for their natural lives?" Those are fair questions, and I do not presume to have a complete answer. I don't know how much the general fallenness and brokenness of our human existence plays into our human physical development, but I *do* know that sometimes the strongest of loves can be wrapped up inside the deepest of pains.

Jessica and I had a special needs child. When our first daughter, Alexis Grace, was born, we were told that she probably would not live through her first year. She had so many medical problems, so many developmental disabilities. She lived to be three-and-a-half, and although we were shattered by her death and the trauma of her agonizing little life, we loved her with a love that we never could have had otherwise. Our love was even sweeter because of the pain.

Jessica and I have spoken with lots of parents of special needs children, and they almost always say the same thing: "This has broken us, and we don't understand it. However, at the same time, wow, this child is a Nathan—they are a gift from God to us." In the middle of our crushing pain with Alexis, I used to thank God that He had allowed me the honor of being her dad. Jessica has spent

---

8. See Jeremiah 1:10

several years working at an elementary school for physically disabled children in Claremont, California, and she routinely marvels how the students can possess such purity, goodness, and beauty in the middle of such challenging, painful lives. Indeed, she has commented that her students often convey a love and a kindness that most people are never able to touch.

I am certainly not trying to minimize the trauma and challenge of physical disability or pain. Nor am I suggesting that a kind disposition somehow makes it all okay. It does not. I am simply saying that sometimes Nathans, or gifts, are present even in the middle of some very crushing, confusing situations.

In her book, *The Spiritual Art of Raising Children with Disabilities*, Kathleen Deyer Bolduc observes that, "No one makes it through this life without experiencing a broken heart. Fragile hearts are a condition of our humanity."[9] She tells the story of a Hassidic rabbi that routinely told his congregation to place the Scripture on their hearts by dutifully studying it. One day, the rabbi was asked about his verbiage—why place the Scripture *on* one's heart instead of *inside* one's heart? He replied, "Only God can put Scripture inside. But reading sacred text can put it on your hearts, and then when your heart breaks, the holy words will fall inside."[10] In her book, *Traveling Mercies: Some Thoughts About Faith*, Anne Lamott quotes poet Eugene O'Neill, "Man is born broken. He lives by mending. The grace of God is glue."[11]

In addition to offering us present-day comfort, the Bible concludes with a powerful reminder that God's intention is to heal and restore everything that is broken or marred. Revelation 21:3–5 states:

> And I heard a loud voice from the throne saying, "Look! God's dwelling place is now among the people, and He will dwell with them. They will be His people, and God Himself will be with them and be their God. He will wipe

9. Bolduc, *The Spiritual Art of Raising Children with Disabilities*, 4.
10. Ibid., 3.
11. Eugene O'Neill, quoted in Anne LaMotte's, *Traveling Mercies: Some Thoughts on Faith*, 112.

every tear from their eyes. There will be no more death or mourning or crying or pain, for the old order of things has passed away." He who was seated on the throne said, "I am making everything new!"

It is almost impossible to live dynamic lives in desperate times until we begin understanding our "before." However, when we understand our before, when we realize that we were envisioned, wanted, loved, and appointed for a purpose, we can get busy loving others and becoming a gift for the world. When we do this, our life comes into sharper focus, a sense of purpose begins to saturate us, and an abiding joy begins to blossom in our soul, despite whatever difficulties surround us.

Is it possible that you need to change your life narrative today and switch to a different, bigger story? Self-discovery is a big deal in the development of infants and toddlers. They say it takes about fifteen to twenty-four months for babies to realize that they are independent of the world around them, they are not just an extension of everything that they see.[12] Although it is a necessary moment for a baby to distinguish him or herself and realize that they are a separate someone, the problem for many of us adults is that we still think that is when it all began for us; yet it did not. It did not begin with self-awareness, and it did not begin by chance. You are not just your DNA. You are more than your upbringing or the product of your parents' union. You are known and loved by Deity. You are God's gift to the world.

Let's reject the lesser narrative. Let's ask God to heal us from our shrunken stories. By faith, let's accept the truth about our before and ask God to make it a reality in our hearts. Finally, let's ask God to show us whose gift we were created to be.

Dynamic lives:

1. Run in a faster heat.

2. Are fueled and sustained by a word from God.

---

12. Dante Cichetti, Marjorie Beeghly, ed., *The Self in Transition: Infancy to Childhood* (Chicago, IL: The University of Chicago Press, 1990), 5.

Your Before

3. Stretch back farther than their family of origin and connect to the "before" of God.

   Questions for Discussion

   - How has your family of origin helped or hindered your understanding of your purpose?
   - When you consider your childhood or young adulthood where do you see glimpses of your ultimate purpose or calling?
   - Who has been a Nathan—a gift—in your life?
   - Whose Nathan is God calling you to be?

Chapter 4

Your Returning

"Return, faithless Israel. . .I will frown on you no longer, for I am faithful. . .I will not be angry forever." (Jeremiah 3:11)

BEFORE YOU STARTED FORMING in your mother's womb, God knew you. Before you were conceived, you already existed in the mind of God. Before your parents hooked up, and regardless of the circumstances surrounding that moment (whether it was true love or a giant mistake for them to be together), God had a plan for you. He wanted you, and He had an appointment for you. Far too many people are living reduced stories that hold them far below their potential because they do not understand their before. They think their before only goes back as far as the night their mom and dad had sex, so if their mom and dad wanted them, then they feel wanted, but if their mom and dad thought their birth was an accident or a mistake, then they feel unsure. If their parents regretted them or considered aborting them or giving them up for adoption or suggested that their birth ruined their lives, those painful wounds can be carried for a lifetime.

Family of origin scars can run very deep and they can affect us for a very long time; consequently, this message from God to Jeremiah (and to you and me) is so healing and powerful. God says, "Before any of that happened, there was an entirely different narrative unfolding." Consider the following scenario.

Imagine a person whose mother or father never learned how to be a real parent. For whatever reason or dysfunction, their mom or dad never stepped up to become a consistent, loving presence or voice; perhaps they were distant and aloof or maybe even damaging or mean. The child in that relationship would understandably grow up doubting his or her legitimacy and questioning whether they were worthy of being loved. But, imagine that one day this child is conducting some family research on a genealogy website and they discover a family legacy that they never knew existed. As they delve deeper, they discover that their great, great, great, great-grandfather was a king or great healer or a wise judge, and they suddenly realize, "Wait a second. There is more to my legacy than the brokenness of my mother and father. There is more to my story than *disowned* or *disappointed*. There's some nobility back there."

Then imagine that they dig a little deeper and they find a published oath or family decree. They learn that their ancestor king had made a proclamation that "Every descendant in this family tree is called to greatness, and no matter what befalls them in their lives, no matter how they are battered and bruised by the storms of life, the daughters and sons of *this house* will always rise and overcome."

Do you think that might add a slightly different perspective? Do you think that might raise the chin of a discouraged child or restore a little swagger to their step? In Isaiah 51:1–2 it says, "Listen to me, you who pursue righteousness and who seek the LORD: Look to the rock from which you were cut and to the quarry from which you were hewn; look to Abraham, your father, and to Sarah, who gave you birth." Isaiah was saying essentially the same thing as Jeremiah.

In Isaiah's day, the northern Kingdom of Israel had so forgotten who they were that they were teetering on the edge of ruin, about to be conquered by Assyria and taken into captivity, so Isaiah pleaded with them, saying basically, "Hey, remember who you really are! You're Abraham's kids! You're Sarah's offspring." Although

Abraham and Sarah had been dead for centuries, Isaiah was trying to remind Israel of their before, reminding them that the whole nation was founded on a promise from God. He was pleading with them to cling to their promises and never forget who they were and whose they were. When we know who we are, when we know that our before stretches clear back to the mind and heart of God, it changes everything. It is sort of like a near-sighted child who puts on prescription glasses for the very first time.

I was nine years old when my parents diagnosed my near-sightedness and bought me my first pair of glasses (they were awesome glasses with flexible hinges and lenses that turned dark in the sun). I still remember driving home from the optometrist's office with my dad and being stunned by all of the detail in the world. I saw the definition of leaves and pine needles for the first time. The clouds were more vivid, and it truly looked like a whole new world. Understanding our before is like that—it's like having our vision come into focus for the very first time.

Wanted

Recently, a woman in my congregation experienced a profound reconnection with her before. This woman was adopted in her infancy and raised by a family who deeply loved her and treated her well; however, questions about her birth parents and the details surrounding her adoption still affected her and plagued her with doubts about her personal legitimacy and worth. In her mid-forties, this woman was married with four natural born children and two adopted children. She and her husband were highly successful and greatly loved. They had tons of friends and were truly the model of a confident, loving family. However, still driven by the questions about her past, she began conducting online family history research.

After several months of exhaustive searching, she had located a pool of family members and decided to make contact with a woman that she suspected of possibly being either an aunt or a distant cousin (the closed terms of her adoption made it nearly impossible to locate more specific family information). She sent a risky email, sharing her story and her quest, and asked the woman if she had any information about her adoptive situation. Amazingly, the woman replied, and her response changed my friend's life forever. It turned out that the woman in question was not an aunt or a distant cousin; she was actually my friend's birth *mom*, and her opening words sent a wave of healing through the miles and the years. She wrote, "I am your mother, and I have been looking for you and longing for you my entire life."

This mom had gotten overwhelmed in college and gave up her daughter for adoption, thinking it was her only option at the time. Later on, she became a Christian, turned her entire life around and ultimately married a pastor and began working in church ministry. She spent time every day praying for the daughter she would never know, trusting that somehow God would intervene and show mercy. It was a healing, triumphant moment when my friend was able to share with her birth mother that she, too, was involved in Christian ministry, that she had adopted children of her own, and that God had indeed been kind. They have since kindled a beautiful relationship and are rapidly making up for lost time.

One particular statement struck me to my core as I was hearing my friend's story. My friend said, "It is crazy to think that I spent my entire life wondering if I was loved and looking for love, when my mom was actually praying for me and loving me the whole time." That's a graphic picture of our situation. Until we connect with our before, we can rush through our lives, trying to find love and belonging in all sorts of places, never knowing that we are loved by Deity the whole time. Let's explore this idea a little further and see what can happen to a person when they don't understand their before.

Lost

In Jeremiah 3:6–10 a scathing, heart-wrenching indictment came from the Lord against the people in Israel:

> During the reign of King Josiah, the LORD said to me, "Have you seen what faithless Israel has done? She has gone up on every high hill and under every spreading tree and has committed adultery there. I thought that after she had done all this she would return to me but she did not, and her unfaithful sister Judah saw it. I gave faithless Israel her certificate of divorce and sent her away because of all her adulteries. Yet I saw that her unfaithful sister Judah had no fear; she also went out and committed adultery. Because Israel's immorality mattered so little to her, she defiled the land and committed adultery with stone and wood. In spite of all this, her unfaithful sister Judah did not return to me with all her heart, but only in pretense," declares the LORD.

This idolatrous activity was occurring during the reign of the good king Josiah. Indeed, by the time he came on the scene and began implementing his revivalist reforms, the country was almost completely given over to idol worship, and Jeremiah's sexual/marital language was used to describe this idolatrous condition. The adultery with sticks and stones was worship that Israel was supposed to be giving to God but instead was giving to man-made idols. The high hills and spreading trees where the people committed adultery were the high places where altars were set up to all kinds of different tribal deities.

Israel's famous She'ma—their famous morning and evening prayer and declaration—said, "Hear O Israel, the LORD your God, the LORD is One. And you shall love the LORD your God with all your heart and soul and with all your might."[1] Unfortunately, Israel had compromised their devotion to the one true God and had embraced the polytheistic syncretism of the nations around them.

This was a tragedy in light of Israel's uniqueness. Israel was the special people of God, called to know Him like no one else ever had. Their before stretched way back to the call of Abraham when he left the idol-worshipping culture of his father and headed out by faith to a new Promised Land. However, when they forgot their

---

1. See Deuteronomy 6:4–5

before, they started looking for it in all of the idolatry and worship rites of the surrounding kingdoms.

Ultimately, they so forgot who their Father really was that this indictment from Jeremiah 2:27 was given: "They say to wood, 'You are my father,' and to stone, 'You gave me birth.'" Please absorb the weight of those words. Israel had been conceived in the mind and dream and promise of Almighty God, they had a special place with Him that no nation had ever known before, and now they were saying to a *stick*, "Are you my dad?" They were saying to a *stone*, "Will you be my father? Can I attach to you? Can I find life on this high place over here?"

Broken Cisterns

Let's switch metaphors for a moment. If we back up to Jeremiah 2:13, we hear God lamenting, "My people have committed two sins: They have forsaken me, the spring of living water, and have dug their own cisterns, broken cisterns that cannot hold water." God said essentially, "Your first problem is that you left me. You cut the cord that anchored you to your before. Then, since you still needed to attach somewhere, you tried attaching to sticks and stones and human things, and the result is like someone who has left a gushing, flowing, artesian well for a leaking cup that cannot hold any water."

This is always the pattern that occurs with sin. The first sin is never the sinful act; it is the fact that we have left the source of life. After we have left it, we then move on to a counterfeit source to try and find life, but it never works for more than a few sips. The leaky cup always dries up, and when it does, we either have to humble ourselves and return to God or go looking for a new cup.

Surely, you have seen this dynamic. You have watched people look for love in all the wrong places. You have seen people trying to attach their identity to things that really cannot satisfy them. Meanwhile, it is painfully obvious to everyone around them: "This person is no good for you! This habit is hurting you. You are only masking your pain; you're not really healing it."

That's what we humans do when we leave the source of life. We over-drink and self-medicate because that is easier than actually engaging with real life. We binge-watch other people living life on television because that is less work than actually getting out there and living ourselves. We turn to porn or other damaging practices because it is easier than cultivating true intimacy with a real human being.

The fundamental problem with these things is not that we are bad people when we engage with them. God's posture is not primarily, "How dare you do those things? Shame on you for self-medicating or over-indulging!" No, rather, it is, "Come back to me! There is an artesian well over here that you can drink from and wash in and find life in, so why are you trying to quench your thirst from a thimble? You have called a stick your father; you've called a stone your source, and it has reduced your world. It's left you empty and inadequate on the inside."

Shrinky Dink Lives

Did you ever play with shrinky dinks when you were a kid? They were really cool activities wherein you would paint a design on a saucer-sized plastic canvas, and then after you were done ascribing your artwork on its surface you would bake the plastic canvas in the oven where it would shrink several times in size. Once shrunken and cooled, your saucer-sized portrait would be small enough to clip to a keychain or even wear around your neck. That's what happens to us when we persist in drinking from the wrong source; it reduces us to a fraction of who we have really been called to be.

Listen to the heart of God in contrast to those moments. Jeremiah 3:12-13 says, "'Return, faithless Israel,' declares the LORD, 'I will frown on you no longer, for I am faithful,' declares the LORD, 'I will not be angry forever.' Only acknowledge your guilt—you have rebelled against the LORD your God." The word "declares" refers to a word or an oracle[2] and is a formal appeal or a declaration from

---

2. Zodhiates, *The Complete Word Study Old Testament*, 1,812, 2,554.

God. In this particular passage, the word comes from a root origin that means, "to whisper."³ So, although God is issuing a formal declaration to His people, He isn't shouting at them. Rather, the passage could read, "'Return to me,' whispers Jehovah." Jeremiah uses *Jehovah*, God's relational, present tense name, in this passage to convey the relational depths of the heart of God.

"*Return to Me,*" *whispers Jehovah.* It is the language of love spoken with the tone of tenderness and intimacy. God is saying, "Come back to me, child. I am here. Quit looking to sticks and stones and inferior sources to attach your destiny to."

Return to Me. That is probably the most recurrent phrase in all of the prophetic messages of the Bible. Nearly all of the Old Testament prophecy books could be summarized this way: "Return to me, my people. The spring water you are looking for is here with me. Come back from the puddle you have been lapping from and live."

Let's move this away from Jeremiah and ancient Israel and let's consider our own lives for a moment. Can you identify any areas where you might be attached to an inferior source? Are you doing any self-medicating instead of going after true healing and resolve? If nothing comes readily to mind, think about someone you love. Is your heart aching for a loved one who keeps persisting in searching for life in dead places?

Shuwb

Here is how we can personally return, and here is how we can pray for our loved ones. In Jeremiah 3:12 God said to Jeremiah, "Go, proclaim this message toward the north, 'Return.'" The word "return" is the Hebrew word *shuwb*, and it contains some powerful, vivid imagery in its definition. *Shuwb*/return means to turn back, to turn oneself, to turn around, to come back to, to turn to Jehovah.⁴ The word sometimes gets translated into English as "recede,"

---

3. Ibid., 1,812, 2,554.
4. Ibid., 1,812, 2,371–2372.

and it speaks of floodwaters returning to where they were before the flood. It is movement back to the point of departure.

To truly understand the scope of the word *shuwb*, picture in your mind a dam, holding back a massive water reserve. Now see that dam straining, cracking, breaking, and then bursting from the buildup of water pressure until all of its water reserves flow away. *Shuwb would be the reversal of that motion*; it would be all of the water receding, like the ocean tide, and moving back to where it was before the dam burst.

Interestingly, in Psalm 23:3 when David says, "He restores my soul" (ESV), the Hebrew word for "restores" is the word *shuwb*. So, David was essentially saying, "When my soul—the totality of my inner man—breaks down and I feel scattered and lost, God gathers up the pieces of my soul and puts me back together again."

If we want to detach from our broken vessels and return—*shuwb*—to God's source of abundant life, there are four steps.

First, start asking God to gather up the fragments of whatever it is you have lost. Wherever you have spread, dabbled, or attached to the wrong places, *shuwb*—return, like floodwaters returning to the point of departure.

Second, while you are asking God to gather up the fragments of everything that's been lost, see God smiling. When we start to *shuwb*, God starts to smile. In Jeremiah 3:12 God said to returning Israel, "I will frown on you no longer." God smiles when we *shuwb* because it means that His children are coming home! The other morning, I was walking outside and praying through a psalm that contained a reference to "sinners" in it. I paused in my walk and said, "Jesus, thank you for dying on the cross for sinners." Immediately, I sensed a reply from the Holy Spirit in my heart, "I didn't die for sinners; I died for sons and daughters."

Certainly we are sinners, and part of the returning process is acknowledging that. However, Jesus did not go to the cross thinking, "Okay, you miserable sinners I will take your place!" Instead, He was looking at daughters and sons, and that is a very different perspective. Cry out to God, ask Him to re-gather the fragments of your soul, and then see Him smiling as you do.

Your Returning

Third, cry "Guilty!" In Jeremiah 12:13, God said, "Only acknowledge your guilt—you have rebelled against the LORD your God." It is pointless to deny our guilt, so, rather than posturing or denying, let's confess it as quickly as we can.

Have you ever watched a high-speed car chase on the news and seen a racing car attempt to outrun police vehicles while a helicopter news crew films the spectacle from above? In those moments, don't you say to yourself, "What are they thinking? Do they really think they are going to get away? Do they think no one knows where they are headed when the whole city is watching them on the evening news?" There is something in the heart of us humans that always thinks we can get away with our rebellious ways, but we can not. We need to pull over. We need to stop the car. We need to cry, Guilty.

Many years ago, I met a pastor from Belfast, Ireland, and he shared how he and his closest friends made it a habit of quickly crying guilty when confronted. When one of them needed to initiate a confrontation or an iron-sharpening-iron moment with someone in the group, the recipient would immediately shoot their hand into the air and cry, "Guilty!"[5] They intentionally practiced being quick to repent, and they learned that it is difficult to condemn a person who so quickly admits their faults. Ask God to re-gather you, see God smiling, and then cry "Guilty!"

Fourth, initiate a breakup. You have probably noticed that in church we tend to focus a lot on whether things are right or wrong or good or bad, and when something lands in the wrong or bad categories, we usually don't have a lot of grace for it. If it is bad, it has to go. Period. I understand why we feel that way, and certainly, we should jettison everything in our lives that separates us from God's life, but there is a problem with that cut-and-dry perspective; it fails to recognize that people can get emotionally attached to things that are not good for them. Did you notice the language that God used in His appeal? It was so personal, intimate, and emotional. God understands that a person's vices can become their friends.

---

5. See Proverbs 27:17

Someone might say, "I know I drink too much. I know I can never stop with just one or two drinks, and when I over-drink I always regret it and pay a price for it. However, I have gone to alcohol for comfort so many times I have relied on it for so long, that it has become my friend. Now, the thought of giving it up and not having it hurts. The thought of letting it go feels almost like a breakup."

At other times, a person might say, "I know this relationship is not good for me, but I have become so attached to it that the process of trying to detach from it is going to cause a tearing, and the tearing is going to hurt."

Now, do we need to ask people to give up some of their vices? Are there certain tearings that need to occur? Of course. Jesus Himself was graphic at times in His instructions to cut out any form of sin from our lives; however, that doesn't mean that we cannot acknowledge the pain while we do. In fact, it actually helps us to do so. Sometimes, breakups are essential, but it can be very helpful to realize that the tearing is indeed a breakup, and it is okay to grieve it. In fact, giving yourself permission to grieve the breakup will actually help you follow through with the breakup. Then, in keeping with the breakup imagery, here are a few points to remember about breakups.

How to Break Up

Sometimes in a breakup one party will say to the other, "It's not you it's me," but when you are detaching from dry and dangerous sources, that is not true. In this case, you must fiercely acknowledge that the inferior source of life is not good for you. Next, remember that you cannot breakup if you keep on dating. It is hard for a dating couple to break up and truly separate if they continue to follow their ex's every online post or comment. Sometimes, clean breaks require clean breaks. Finally, we need to trust that our new relationship will be better; our new source will be superior.

If God is better, God *will be* better. The problem with too many Christian stories is that they sound like this: "God worked in my life, I finally surrendered to Him, and then I gave up all of my old friends and vices." When I hear people say things like that, I always want to ask, "Yes, and then what happened? Surely, that's not the end of the story. What did you replace those things with? What did you re-attach to?"

When we ask people to give up things that they love, we cannot leave them thinking that their only option is a painful amputation. God forbid! We need to help them detach so they can reattach to something far superior. This whispering, wooing, loving God is *vastly* superior to anything that we give up in order to have more of Him, and He is beckoning us to run toward Him and do a cannonball into the river of the Spirit of God. A towering life is a life that draws its life from authentic sources of life. You and I will never live towering, terrific lives if we are holding onto our inferior attachments. We need to *shuwb*. We need to return.

Dynamic lives:

1. Run in a faster heat.
2. Are fueled and sustained by a word from God.
3. Stretch back farther than their family of origin and connect to the "before" of God.
4. Are quick to *shuwb*/return.

Questions for Discussion

- Have you ever tried to draw life from lifeless sources?
- Are there any areas of your life where you are attempting to do that today? If so, how is that working out for you?
- Do you remember shrinky dinks? Can you see how attaching to the wrong source shrinks the life of God in you?
- Are you ready to *shuwb*/return to God's ultimate source?

CHAPTER 5

Prophetic People

"I appointed you as a prophet to the nations." (Jeremiah 1:5)

HAVE YOU EVER BEEN in a setting where someone was telling you about their life, or you were watching them *live* their life, and you felt like you could see their future a little more clearly than they could? Have you ever looked at someone and either thought or said, "Even if you can't perceive it right now, I can clearly see where this path is taking you"? Sometimes that path is a negative one where we can see potential danger in someone's future, and sometimes it is positive. People often cannot see their own potential, and they need outside voices to speak to their talents or their calling. Have you ever had either a positive or a negative premonition about someone's future before they could see it for themselves?

If so, you have likely touched the prophetic word.

Very simply, a prophetic word is a word that God is speaking *now*. Prophecy is not necessarily futuristic, as it is not always forecasting or fortune-telling. Rather, Biblical prophecy is forth telling, proclaiming a word that God is speaking *now*.[1] And He

---

1. Steven L. McKenzie, "Forthtelling, Not Foretelling," *Oxford Scholarship Online*, September 2011, accessed January 26, 2018, http://www.oxfordscholarship.com/view/10.1093/acprof:oso/9780195161496.001.0001/

is speaking now. God is not the cosmic watchmaker who set the world in motion and then silently stepped back to watch things run their course.

Deism is a belief in a cosmic watchmaker God who created and assembled all of the elements of our universe and then wound everything up, set it all in motion, and then backed away. Oxford's online dictionary defines deism as "Belief in the existence of a supreme being, specifically of a creator who does not intervene in the universe."[2] For a Deist, God definitely exists but He is not actively involved in His creation. A Deist, therefore, would rarely ever say, "God spoke to me." On the opposite extreme from a distant, deistic view of God would be people who say that God speaks to them on the hour about even the tiniest details of their lives. Some people believe that God tells them what to wear in the morning or how they should part their hair. Certainly, God *can* and maybe sometimes *does* speak to people that way; however, I love a more balanced approach that I once heard from my favorite preacher, Dr. Syvelle Phillips.

I'm Not Your Mother!

Dr. Phillips had attended a seminar on the subject of hearing God's voice, and the speaker regaled her audience with stories of how God routinely spoke to her about the daily details of her life, including the selection of her outfits in the morning. Dr. Phillips was deeply moved and desirous of hearing God's voice at that same level, so he decided to try it. The next morning, he thought, "I want God to speak to me the way He speaks to that teacher," so he stood in front of his open closet, surveying his array of pants and shirts, and he asked the Lord, "God, which of these outfits do you want me to wear today?" Then he paused to listen.

---

acprof-9780195161496-chapter-3.

2. Oxford Dictionaries Online. Accessed January 26, 2018. http://wwwen.oxforddictionaries.com/definition/deism.

After a moment, he clearly sensed the Spirit speaking to his heart. God said, "I'm not your mother! I trust you to get dressed in the morning."

A little later in the same day, Dr. Phillips was at a car lot, shopping for a newer car, and he again paused to pray, "Lord, would you give me wisdom and direct me to the perfect car." Again, the voice of the Holy Spirit echoed through his soul: "Son, I'm not your mother. I trust you to make a wise decision about your monthly budget."

The point of Dr. Phillips' story is not a mockery or a disparaging of those who yearn to hear God's voice in the smaller details of their lives. God can certainly speak to those things; however, when we discuss the leading or guidance of the Spirit, we need to avoid the extremes of both cynical deism or irresponsible mysticism. The reality probably lies somewhere in the middle: God most definitely speaks, but we must handle His word, and our interpretations of those words, with great care, never flippantly or presumptuously.

God Speaks

The fact that God speaks is a foundational idea in Christianity. God speaks:

Through the still, small voice in our souls (1 Kings 19:12; Isaiah 30:21).

Through dreams and visions (Job 33:14–18; Acts 10:3–6, 9–15).

Through creation and nature (Psalm 19:1–4; Romans 1:20).

Through the people that God has placed in our lives (Hebrews 13:7).

Through Jesus, His Son (Hebrews 1:1–2).

And through the Scriptures (2 Timothy 3:15–17).

When Jesus spoke of shepherds and sheep in John 10:4, He said that sheep follow their shepherd because they know his voice. He went on to say in verse 14, "I am the good shepherd; I know my sheep and my sheep know me." He knows us and we are able to know Him in kind through the words that He reveals to us.

Prophetic People

As we attempt to discern God's voice for today, we first understand that He has already spoken to us through the Scriptures (we call that "special revelation"), and the words that He speaks today will confirm and reinforce the Scripture.[3] This is crucial: what God *has* spoken and what God *is* speaking are intimately connected. Additionally, by understanding what *has been spoken* we can usually deduce what is probably *being spoken*. For instance, Jessica and I have been married for twenty-three years, and throughout those years she has written me numerous notes and cards (as well as a few "come to Jesus" letters). I have kept almost every one, and based on what she has written me in the past, combined with how she has consistently lived her life, I can usually deduce with reasonably strong accuracy what she is most likely to think or say about a given situation. I can usually tell what she will say to me today based on what she has been saying to me for over two decades.

I should also mention, however, that even though I can often anticipate what Jessica will think or feel about a situation, she is not a one-dimensional, predictable being. I am in a living breathing relationship with a *person*, not an idea or a formula or an equation. Even though I remember what she *has* spoken (and by knowing what she has spoken I can probably guess what she *will* say) sometimes I need more than what *has been* spoken; I need what *is being spoken*. Sometimes I need to hear what is being spoken even if it is identical to something that has already been said.

In marriage ministry, I am always shocked and I have to laugh when someone says to his or her spouse, "I told you I loved you when I married you; why do I need to keep saying it and expressing it?" The answer is obvious: even if today's word is exactly the same as yesterday's word, sometimes we need to hear it again *today*. When I need real-time affirmation from Jessica, a twenty-year old card does not cut it. The same is also true with God.

---

3. Elwell, *Baker's Evangelical Dictionary of Biblical Theology*.

Reminders

I love the sentiment that the Apostle Paul expressed to the church in Philippi when he wrote, "It is no trouble for me to write the same things to you again, and it is a safeguard for you" (Philippians 3:1). Paul did not say, "I've already told you this stuff—why do I have to keep repeating it?" Rather, he said, "I would love to remind you of this word—in fact, it is good for you to be reminded of it."

So prophecy is a "now" word from God that takes the essence of what *has been* spoken and brings it into the immediacy of today. Also, many people are far more prophetic than they realize. Consider the following. How do you respond when someone comes to you in a heartbroken or discouraged state? You naturally begin prophesying to them! You say, "Oh I'm so sorry; I know that hurts. I know this is a tough time, but I promise you God is still for you, and He can bring good even into the middle of this heartbreak."

What do you communicate when someone is distraught over a terrible failure or regret in their life? Again, you prophesy—you speak forth God's sentiment, "Yes, sin is the worst, isn't it? It brings death, every time. But, thank God sin never has the final word. Jesus absorbed our sin. He paid the price for us, and the clearest picture we have of God's heart for us is Jesus Christ dying on behalf of us sinners and then inviting us to step into His new life."

Additionally, someone may confide in you, "My relationship is all jacked up and we can never seem to get it together." After you dig around a little bit and ask a few probing questions, you suddenly get clarity and say, "Hold on, the problem is that you keep relating based on a flawed system. There is a whole different way of living, relating, serving, and loving than what you are currently practicing. There is a different path to follow, and if you follow it, healing will happen." That's prophetic! All of those expressions of counsel are real-time expressions of the word and reality of God for a given situation.

It is interesting to note that in both the Old and New Testaments both Moses and the Apostle Paul expressed a desire for every single member of God's family to prophesy. In Numbers 11:25–29, Moses said:

> Then the LORD came down in the cloud and spoke with him, and he took some of the power of the Spirit that was on him and put it on the seventy elders. When the Spirit rested on them, they prophesied—but did not do so again. However, two men, whose names were Eldad and Medad, had remained in the camp. They were listed among the elders, but did not go out to the tent. Yet the Spirit also rested on them, and they prophesied in the camp. A young man ran and told Moses, "Eldad and Medad are prophesying in the camp." Joshua son of Nun, who had been Moses' aide since youth, spoke up and said, "Moses, my lord, stop them!" But Moses replied, "Are you jealous for my sake? I wish that all the LORD's people were prophets and that the LORD would put his Spirit on them!"

In 1 Corinthians 14:5, the Apostle Paul wrote, "I would like every one of you to speak in tongues, but I would rather have you prophesy." Paul wanted every Christian to prophesy because prophetic ministry contains a life-changing power. In verse 3, Paul explained, "The one who prophesies speaks to people for their strengthening, encouraging and comfort." Wow, don't you want to be associated with that kind of church? Don't you want to belong to a place where "strength, encouragement, and comfort" are the oxygen and ethos of the group?

All About Jesus

Ultimately, prophetic ministry is all about Jesus Christ. In Revelation 19:10, it says that, "the testimony of Jesus is the spirit of prophecy" (KJV). A true prophetic word illuminates, amplifies, and glorifies the heart, work, and person of Jesus Christ, and it calls us to walk more closely with Him and His purposes for our lives.

When I was nineteen years old, I went to a church service to hear a guest speaker, and at the end of his message he extended an offer to pray for anyone who wanted to receive some personal ministry. However, before he did so, he called a few specific individuals up front to pray for them publicly (I was one of them). Although I had never met this man before, he looked at me for a few seconds and then he said, "Lord, thank you for the pastoral calling that's on this young man's life." When he said that I looked up at him and began shaking my head. I had no plans to be a pastor. My self-identified dream was to become a high school English teacher, a novelist, and a track and field coach. When this minister saw me shaking my head, he said, "And Lord would you adjust this man to receive the calling that you've placed on him?"

Something changed in me, not immediately and not that night, but in that season of my life. Multiple events began occurring to get my attention and confirm for me that I was *not* called to teach in a school setting, but rather I was called to teach in a *church* setting; I was called to be a pastor. May I share with you the entire word that he gave me? It included a word from Jeremiah 3:15 where God said to Israel, "I will give you shepherds after my own heart." This is what that man prophesied over me:

> Lord, I thank you for the pastoral anointing that is upon this young man's life, and that in the years to come you will put upon him the heart of a shepherd, and that it would align with the Scripture that says, "In the last days, I will raise up shepherds after my own heart." It may not be in the traditional sense that most people think of pastoring but it will be in the sense of caring for the sheep and loving the sheep and ministering to the sheep. Lord, I thank you, and as I pray for him, I prophesy the pastoral care that's going to be upon his life—the spirit of wisdom, the spirit of counsel and might and the spirit of the Lord—will be such that he will be able to minister to those who need to be healed from the bruising they have received from the cares of this world. Lord, we adjust this man right now to receive the call that you have placed upon his life.

Prophetic People

My encounter with the prophetic word that night set me on a course that changed my life forever.

Like Jeremiah before us, you and I have a two-fold word from God as well: one is a word for us to personally embrace and live, and the other is a word for us to carry to someone else. When we discover, embrace, and export our word, dynamic living begins in earnest.

Dynamic lives:

1. Run in a faster heat.
2. Are fueled and sustained by a word from God.
3. Stretch back farther than their family of origin and connect to the "before" of God.
4. Are quick to *shuwb*/return.
5. Carry a prophetic word from the Lord for others.

Questions for Discussion

- How have you understood prophetic ministry in the past?
- Have you ever considered yourself to be prophetic?
- Moses and Paul would like you to prophesy—would you be willing to ask God to use you prophetically?
- How do we use what *has been* spoken (special revelation) to help us perceive what *is being* spoken?

Chapter 6

Carrier of Hope Proclaimer of Judgment

"The word of the LORD came to me: 'What do you see, Jeremiah?'
'I see the branch of an almond tree...I see a pot that is boiling.'"
(Jeremiah 1:11, 13)

JEREMIAH WAS A PROPHET—THAT'S a *noun*.

You and I are probably not nouns; we are probably *adjectives*. Jeremiah was a prophet, but we are most likely prophet-*ic*—we know that we are called to speak words of strength, encouragement, and comfort to people, but we don't necessarily feel called to give ourselves to a lifetime of prophetic ministry. Some people do. Some people feel called to a more formal, official role of prophetic ministry, but most us will minister more like adjectives. That is what the Apostle Paul was referencing when he said, "The one who prophesies speaks to people for their strengthening, encouraging and comfort," and again, "I would like every one of you to speak in tongues, but I would rather have you prophesy."[1] Whether we feel called as nouns or adjectives, we have all been invited into the power and wonder of carrying and speaking God's encouraging, prophetic words of life for other people.

---

1. See 1 Corinthians 14:3, 5

CARRIER OF HOPE PROCLAIMER OF JUDGMENT

In contrast to an unquestioning embrace of today's political, culturally acceptable way of living, prophetic ministry awakens deeper, truer passions in people's hearts. Prophetic ministers encourage their hearers to feel deeply, to question the status quo, and to drink deeply of God's reality amid all of the highs and lows of life. Brueggemann pointedly states, "We need to ask if our consciousness and imagination have been so assaulted and co-opted. . .that we have been robbed of the courage or power to think an alternative thought."[2] Brueggemann uses the term "world-weariness" to describe the state of Christians who have become so immersed in today's frantic culture that they have lost their vision of real life inside God's kingdom, and from both my personal experiences and my observations of other people, it is a fitting description. The people I minister to are often world-weary, overwhelmed by information, and stressed from overtaxed schedules and shrinking margins, as well as the general pressures of busy, North American living.

Consider this assessment of American culture from a foreign observer in 1962:

> You call your thousand material devices, "labor-saving machinery," yet you are forever "busy." With the multiplying of your machinery you grow increasingly fatigued, anxious, nervous, dissatisfied. Whatever you have, you want more; and wherever you are you want to go somewhere else. Your devices are neither time-saving nor soul-saving machinery. You are the most nervously busy man in the world.[3]

If that assessment was true in the 1960s, it is certainly true today, as the pace of life has continued to accelerate. On a regular basis, I hear people lament that they are either too tired or busy for church attendance, or that spiritual matters are becoming less important to them in light of all the other demands they face. Whether this can be blamed on the frenetic pace of modern living, people's misplaced priorities and devotion, the increasing

---

2. Brueggemann, *The Prophetic Imagination*, 39.
3. King Jr., *Strength to Love*, 75–76.

irrelevance of the today's church, or other spiritual factors, it must be countered by creative, authentic prophetic ministry.

God's Word to The Mountains

In the Old Testament, both Isaiah and Micah prophetically declared that, "The mountain of the Lord's temple will be established as the highest of the mountains, it will be exalted above the hills, and all nations will stream to it."[4] This powerfully imagery reminds us that God's word extends beyond mere personal messages of prophecy to words for entire nations. The prophetic voice has always spoken to kings and empires as well as to individuals and families. Although the emphasis of this book is on helping us walk in step with God's word for our personal lives, I would be remiss to not mention that prophetic ministry reaches much further than that.

God's word reaches into politics, education, and law. It reaches into issues of economics, justice, and social reform. Indeed, it reaches into every other mountain, every other center of influence in our world today. God has a word and wisdom for every aspect of human existence, and He is still calling Jeremiah's to stand in those places and speak His word there.

Not Too Young

When God initially called Jeremiah into prophetic ministry, the young man responded similarly to how you or I might respond. He said, "Alas, Sovereign LORD. . .I do not know how to speak; I am too young" (Jeremiah 1:6). In light of the weightiness of a subject like prophetic ministry, we might feel that way too. We might not think we are too young *physically*, but we might assume that we are too young *spiritually*. We may think, "I don't know enough about God or the Bible to presume to prophesy to someone." Or, we may feel that our spiritual education or training is deficient, and we

---

4. See: Isaiah 2:2; Micah 4:1

wouldn't trust ourselves to prophesy: "I don't want to tell someone 'this is a word from God' when it might just be a word from my own imagination." Certainly, that caution is good and humble and wise, and yet, despite those concerns, Paul still told New Testament believers, "I want you *all* to prophesy."

It makes sense that Jeremiah felt overwhelmed by this calling and sensed his own youthfulness and inexperience because God *always* calls people to tasks that are too big for them. Possibly, the most misquoted idea from Scripture is the idea that "God will never give you anything that you can't handle." Have you heard that sentiment? It is nowhere in the Bible. When it comes to areas of temptation and enticement to sin, yes, God promises, "No temptation has overtaken you except what is common to mankind. And God is faithful; He will not let you be tempted beyond what you can bear. But when you are tempted, He will also provide a way out so that you can endure it."[5] However, when it comes to facing daunting tasks and carrying heavy burdens, we merely need to look at David, Moses, Joshua, Mary, or John and we will readily see that God often gives people more than they can handle on their own. The promise is not, "You can handle it," but rather, "I will handle it with you."

Moses never could have parted the Red Sea unless God stood beside him on the seashore. Goliath would likely have killed young David if God had not put His weight behind David's sling and stone. Nor did Jeremiah possess the ability to prophesy to nations; however, that was okay—God was going to speak through him.

In this Christ-oriented life, it is never a valid excuse to say, "God, I can't obey you because this assignment is too big for me." We will *always* face situations too big for us to handle, and if we face them on our own they will inevitably squash us. However, God promises to face them with us. Towering, dynamic lives are not lived in our own strength; they are lived in sync with the help that God Himself promises to provide.

When my daughters, Amber and Madelyn, were very small I asked them to help me move a sofa into another room. They

---

5. See 1 Corinthians 10:13

looked at the oversized piece of furniture and wailed, "That's way too big, there is no way we can move that!" They hadn't considered the fact that I would be lifting it with them; indeed, I would be doing nearly all of the lifting. Their portion would simply be to help me balance it a little while I walked. In the exact moment that God called Jeremiah into the prophetic office, He also assured Jeremiah that He would help him.

"The LORD said to me, 'Do not say, "I am too young." You must go to everyone I send you to and say whatever I command you. Do not be afraid of them, for I am with you and will rescue you,' declares the LORD" (Jeremiah 1:7-8). This response from God highlights a noteworthy truth: *Feelings of inadequacy only have one source: the wrong reliance.* We think our assignment is too great because we view it through the lens of our personal competencies or inadequacies; we compare our puny muscles to the giant boulder that God is calling us to move. Jeremiah was correct: he was very young and his prophetic calling was very daunting; however, God never told him to pursue it on his own. God Himself was going to put His words in Jeremiah's mouth, and the first word that God gave Jeremiah came in the form of a vision. In Jeremiah 1:11-13, he said, "The word of the LORD came to me: 'what do you see, Jeremiah?' 'I see the branch of an almond tree...I see a pot that is boiling...it is tilting toward us from the north.'"

Almond Branches and Boiling Pots

What a peculiar introductory vision. Although I love almonds, I would never have predicted that the very first vision God would give to Jeremiah would be the picture of an almond blossom or a boiling pot tilting from the north. What is up with that? Why would God show Jeremiah these images in his young, initial prophetic encounter?

Here in Southern California, we take springtime blossoms for granted because something is always blooming. We do not really experience a winter death here in The Golden State. However, in eastern Washington where I grew up, the winters were harsh and long, and the appearance of the first springtime blossom was amazing (I still remember the elation I felt as a boy when spring would break through and I could spot patches of earth appearing from beneath the melting snow). In colder parts of the country with severe winters, the first blossom of spring is a profound harbinger of better days, and it was the same in the agricultural region of Palestine in Jeremiah's day.

In *Run with The Horses*, Eugene Peterson observed that, "The almond tree is one of the earliest trees to bloom in Palestine."[6] Consequently, the appearance of an almond blossom was a prophetic promise that life, harvest, and abundance were re-emerging after the death that comes in winter. So, the very first thing that God wanted Jeremiah to see was a promise of spring. That is the promise embodied in an almond blossom: spring is on the way; warmer days are coming; songbirds will be reappearing soon. It is like a visual picture of the promise from Psalm 30:5 that says, "Weeping may stay for the night, but rejoicing comes in the morning." Indeed, tears may have spent the night with you, but there is a new houseguest coming with the dawn.

The first role of a prophet is to remind people that God brings life out of death, that there *is* an end to winter. Perhaps as you read this, you need a springtime word. Perhaps you need to see your own vision of a blossoming almond branch, or perhaps a co-worker or someone in your sphere of influence needs to see one. Maybe you are their prophet. Maybe you are called to be their Jeremiah. The prophet's primary job is to remind people that God brings new life out of seasons of loss. Springtime is coming.

After Jeremiah saw God's promise of spring, God said, well done. "The LORD said to me, 'You have seen correctly, for I am watching to see that my word is fulfilled'" (Jeremiah 1:12). Then God said, "What else do you see?" and Jeremiah replied, "I see a pot that is boiling. . .it is tilting toward us from the north" (Jeremiah 1:13).

I have never experienced a prayer time like that one. I have never gone into a time of prayer and then come out with pictures of

6. Peterson, *Run with The Horses*, 53.

almond branches and boiling pots in my head. Nor would I be able to understand what Jeremiah was seeing if God hadn't explained it to him. In verses 14–16, He explained: "From the north disaster will be poured out on all who live in the land. . .I will pronounce my judgments on my people because of their wickedness in forsaking me, in burning incense to other gods and in worshipping what their hands have made."

The first role of a prophet is to remind people that spring is coming. The second role is to warn them about God's judgment.

God's Judgment

God's judgment is a pervasive theme throughout Scripture. Have you noticed when you are checking out movie ratings that sometimes a particular film carries the warning: "Rated R for pervasive language"? Judgment is a pervasive biblical theme and it is *not* limited to the Old Testament. Sometimes people wrongly think that the Old Testament God was uptight and quick to judge, but then He somehow got therapy during the inter-testamental period and then came back in the New Testament as Jesus who was all about love and being non-judgmental.

Actually, judgment is a theme in *both* parts of the Bible. In Acts 24:25, when the New Testament recounts the Apostle Paul's trial before the Roman Governor Felix, it says, "As Paul talked about righteousness, self-control and the judgment to come, Felix was afraid." The idea of judgment is understandably uncomfortable and it makes us afraid, but that is because we often do not fully understand it.

When I have asked people, "What is God's judgment?" they have typically replied, "Judgment is an expression of the anger and punishment that God brings against us when we disobey Him. God gets mad when we are bad, and if we are bad enough He will judge us. When He judges us He is actively punishing us." Although variations of that sentiment often get applied to the doctrine of divine judgment, it is not exactly correct.

CARRIER OF HOPE PROCLAIMER OF JUDGMENT

Father Not Judge

Out of all possible metaphors that God could have used in Scripture to reveal Himself to us, consider which was the most prevalent. Out of the many dozens of names for God in the Bible, Jesus said that when we pray to God we should address Him as "Father."[7] Parenthood at its absolute best (not at its human, dysfunctional worst) gives us the clearest idea of what God is like. In the Sermon on the Mount, Jesus said, "If you, then, though you are evil, know how to give good gifts to your children, how much more will your Father in heaven give good gifts to those who ask him!"[8] Jesus was saying essentially, "If you want to know what God is like, imagine the best parent you have ever seen and then multiply their heart, love, goodness, and devotion exponentially."

That is the kind of God who speaks of judgment in the Scriptures.

Having recognized that, now imagine how a loving, committed parent would speak to a child who refuses to listen or obey, and who persists in going down paths that the parent knows are hazardous for them. What kinds of things would that parent say? What would their tone be?

If you are not a parent, or if you are a parent that has not experienced these kinds of dynamics with your child, please try to imagine the weight of the emotion, trauma, and angst that you would feel if you had a child that hardened their heart toward you and insisted on following destructive life paths. What would you feel and communicate if your precious child refused your counsel and persisted in making damaging, ruinous decisions? What would you say to your best friend, relative, or sweetheart if they did the same?

If you *have* experienced dynamics like these, then you understand some of the accompanying emotion, heartache, desperation, and pain. Additionally, you also understand the vast majority of the judgment passages in the Bible. Throughout Israel's history,

---

7. See Matthew 6:9
8. See Matthew 6:11

God's people were fickle in their allegiance to Him, and they constantly pursued idolatrous passions and destructive, forbidden paths. Since God is the paragon of parental love, it makes sense that He would feel extreme waves of parental emotion when His children walked away from Him like that.

Sometimes, the Old Testament prophecy books can be confusing, because in one verse God pleads with Israel like a heartbroken sweetheart, but then in another verse He sounds like a ticked off parent. Later, He sounds sad and grieved again, eventually saying things like, "If you persist in this decision, judgment will overtake you, and you will come to ruin! Return to me and live; refuse me and judgment is coming." This is the essence of the Old Testament prophecy books in one sentence: God is a parent, expressing all of the parental passion and pathos to His children who keep walking away from Him.

It is also very important to note that in the majority of judgment passages in the Bible, God is not actively smiting people because He is angry at them. He is simply allowing the consequences of their choices to fall on them. This concept could fill an entire volume, but let me state it in a simple sentence: God's judgment is not primarily an expression of His active punishment; rather, it is His heartbroken withdrawal and allowance for people's choices to bring about their in-built consequences. Author and apologist Gregory A. Boyd remarks, "God doesn't *impose* punishments on people. The destructive consequences of sin are *built into the sin itself*. And this is why God only needs to withdraw and let sin run its self-destructive course when He judges people."[9] Boyd calls sin "self-punishing" and he describes God's judgment as "divine abandonment" wherein He allows us to choose the consequences of that sin.[10]

I watch this happen all the time. People make foolish decisions that cause them grief or pain, and then they ask, "Why is God punishing me?" People sin and live outside of God's prescribed

---

9. Boyd, *Cross Vision: How the Crucifixion of Jesus Makes Sense of Old Testament Violence*, 148.

10. Ibid., 147.

CARRIER OF HOPE PROCLAIMER OF JUDGMENT

path and then they get confused and disoriented when things don't work out and they lament, "Why would God let this happen to me?" The reality is that God is not punishing; He is not judging. When we walk away from the path of life and insist on more destructive roads, there are consequences. The father of the Prodigal Son never actively punished the son, but he did allow him to leave until circumstances judged him and brought him back home.[11]

God is not an angry, ticked off deity. He is a parent, a best friend, and a spouse, and His communications throughout the prophetic books of the Bible reflect the passion and the pathos of those roles. The first role of a prophet is to bring a springtime word of hope about God's faithfulness; the second is to plead with people to never leave Him, but rather to stay on the paths that lead to life.

Judgment Is Contained

Notice something else about Jeremiah's second vision. Yes, judgment was being poured out, as in the symbolism of the boiling liquid, but it was being poured out of a *pot*. Judgment was coming, but it was *contained*; there were limits to it. God did not show Jeremiah a boiling ocean; He showed him a small, boiling container. Israel had indeed run away from God, and whenever people run from Him they invite in-built consequences into their lives. However, judgment is not infinite; it is a tool that God uses when all other appeals have been rejected, and even then, there is hope. Peterson observes, "The boiling pot reduces evil to a location and a use."[12] The boiling pot is just a pot—it is not an ocean. The ocean is God's *love*.

How to Do It

Since part of our dynamic living includes an element of prophetic ministry, let me close this chapter with three suggestions about

---

11. See Luke 15:11–32
12. Peterson, *Run with The Horses*, 55.

how we should minister prophetically, especially when our prophetic messages include words of warning.

Pray first; speak second. Whenever we feel that we are receiving a word from God, our immediate response should be prayer, not an instantaneous blurting out. It is interesting to note that the very first time the word "prophet" is used in the Bible, it was applied by God to Abraham in a context of prayer. God spoke to King Abimelek and said that Abraham, a prophet, would pray for him so that he and his household could be healed.[13] Applying the Bible study principle of the Law of First Mention, we see that the principal task of a prophet is not *prophesying* it is *praying*.[14] Pray first speak second.

Weep first; speak second. The intensity of God's judgment appeals flows out of the intensity of His love. If He did not care, He would not agonize over our decisions, and it is the same with us in our human relationships. If I love you enough to cry my eyes out for you, then I am possibly qualified to warn you. Jeremiah is known traditionally as "the weeping prophet" because of verses like Jeremiah 9:1, where he cried, "Oh, that my head were a spring of water and my eyes a fountain of tears! I would weep day and night for the slain of my people." When a person loves enough to weep day and night over someone, they are probably qualified to issue a warning, and their warning will likely be pure.

Be observant. Pay attention to inner promptings, leadings of the Holy Spirit, and *déjà vu* moments. When you experience those, pray! Perhaps the inward nudge is a precursor for a word from God, so remain thoughtful and aware. Also, be sure to look people in the eye and notice their reactions and expressions. It is remarkable that Joseph's release from the Pharaoh's prison came about simply because he observed a particular sadness on the faces of two of his fellow prisoners. He asked them why they were sad,

---

13. See Genesis 20:17

14. The Law of First Mention is a Bible interpretation rule that sees the first Scriptural mention of a doctrine or concept as definitive—first mentions often reveal fundamental, inherent meanings. See Dr. F.E. Marsh's, *The Structural Principles of the Bible* (John Ritchie Ltd., 2008).

and the ensuing prophetic interactions ultimately led to his release from jail and his promotion to the second highest leadership role in the entire nation of Egypt.[15]

Once when I was in college, I was standing in the back of a long line at my bank, and I noticed that my pastor was standing in front of a window, conversing with a teller. Of course, I couldn't tell what they were discussing, but I noticed that the teller eventually began to cry and had to wipe away tears that were sliding down her cheeks. Later on, I asked my pastor about the interaction, and he said simply, "I noticed that she looked sad, so I asked if she was okay, and I told her I would pray."

Let's be observant. Let's look for sad faces, and let's be ready carriers of a springtime message from God. Let's not fear this ministry. We are called to be adjectives, prophetic messengers, conveying God's love, light, hope, and wisdom to our world. Life gets exciting when we begin to do so.

Dynamic lives:

1. Run in a faster heat.
2. Are fueled and sustained by a word from God.
3. Stretch back farther than their family of origin and connect to the "before" of God.
4. Are quick to *shuwb*/return.
5. Carry a prophetic word from the Lord for others.
6. Are carriers of hope and proclaimers of judgment—they remind people that spring is coming, and they constantly call people back to their place in God.

Questions for Discussion

- Are you an adjective or a noun?
- Whose Jeremiah are you called to be? Who in your sphere of influence needs to hear a springtime word?

---

15. See Genesis 40–41

- Did this chapter help your understanding of God's judgment? Have you ever experienced the in-built consequences of walking away from God?
- Are you overwhelmed by any challenges in your life because you are viewing them primarily through the perspective of your own human abilities, rather than God's?

CHAPTER 7

The Ancient Path

"This is what the LORD says, 'Stand at the crossroads and look; ask for the ancient paths, ask where the good way is, and walk in it, and you will find rest for your souls'."
(Jeremiah 6:16)

HAVE YOU EVER NEEDED to find rest for your soul? Have you ever gotten weary on the *inside*?

We've all gotten weary on the outside. We have all become so tired at times that we fell asleep when we were supposed to be awake. Sometimes, students fall asleep in class. Sometimes, church members fall asleep in church. Sadly, for my wife, I fall asleep in almost every movie that we watch at night.

Have you ever pulled an all-nighter or battled with jet lag from traveling in an international time zone? Isn't it amazing how missing just one night of sleep can mess us up so badly? And how about insomnia? Insomnia is a form of suffering, isn't it? When someone suffers from chronic insomnia, it feels like torture. In fact, sleep deprivation has been used as actual torture for hundreds of years, and even though it may seem a little more humane than other forms of torture (poking a person when they nod off may seem kinder than physically beating them), sleep deprivation is very damaging.

Dynamic Living in Desperate Times

Prolonged sleep deprivation can cause cognitive impairment, it can break down willpower, and sometimes it can even lead to psychosis, where emotions get so impaired that there is an actual break from reality. It can weaken immune systems and can eventually cause heart defects and cardiovascular disease.[1] One of the primary reasons sleep deprivation gets used as a form of torture is because the deprivation lowers resistance to physical pain (it is poignant to note that Jesus was awake all night—sleep deprived—before His severe beatings and tortures began). Additionally, sleep deprivation makes a person more vulnerable to suggestions and outside influences.[2]

So, think about this: if we can get tired enough on the outside that it can damage our organs, intellect, immune system, and our emotional and mental health, what happens when we get that tired on the *inside*, in our soul? What happens to us when our souls get fatigued? Do you think it is possible that the external crisis of fatigue that our bodies experience can also be reflected on the inside with our souls?

Proverbs 13:12 seems to suggest so. It tells us that "Hope deferred makes the heart sick." It seems that if the human soul gets too tired, too disappointed, discouraged, or low, it will eventually get sick. Have you had any hope-deferred disappointments this year? Have any of your relationships suffered recently? Do any of your dreams remain unfulfilled? Have you carried heavy burdens for a lot longer than you thought you would have to carry them? Are you stuck in any prolonged seasons of disappointment?

Fatigue-induced soul sickness can become a crisis. Fortunately, Jesus understood this. He was concerned about soul fatigue, and in Matthew 11:28-29 He said, "Come to me, all you who are weary and burdened, and I will give you rest. Take my yoke upon

---

1. C. Marzano, M. Ferrara, G. Curcio, & L. Gennaro, L (2010). "The effects of sleep deprivation in humans: Topographical electroencephalogram changes in non-rapid eye movement (NREM) sleep versus REM sleep," *Journal of Sleep Research*, 19(2), (2010): 260-268.

2. Kayt Sukel, "Sleep Deprivation Increases Susceptibility to False Memories," *Dana.org*, accessed January 22, 2018, http://www.dana.org/News/sleep_Deprivation_Increases_Susceptibility_to_False_Memories/.

you and learn from me, for I am gentle and humble in heart, and you will find rest for your souls." That sounds a lot like the verse from the beginning of this chapter, doesn't it? It sounds like keeping company with Jesus will take us onto an ancient path where our souls can finally rest.

In Hebrew the word "rest" usually refers to a resting *place*, but sometimes the word also includes the idea of "poetry" in it.[3] So, this resting place of God is a place where the poetry gets renewed in our soul. The daily pressures and grind of life can easily drain the poetry from our souls, but God's rest restores it.

In Greek the word "rest" (*anapausō*) refers to an intermission or a cessation from work so that one can engage in recreation.[4] And please note that recreation is different from entertainment. We can be entertained for hours and not be affected at all in our souls. However, true recreation does more than entertain or amuse us; it re-creates us. Recreation is activity that re-creates us on the inside so that our soul can discern life's poetry again. A synonym of the word *anapausō* is *anapsuxis*, and it refers to a much-needed recovery of one's breath.[5]

Where It Happens

This poetic, re-creation of our souls occurs as we keep company with Jesus on the ancient pathways. "This is what the LORD says: 'Stand at the crossroads and look; ask for the ancient paths, ask where the good way is, and walk in it, and you will find rest for your souls'" (Jeremiah 6:16). Others have walked these paths before us and have found life, hope, and healing there. Fortunately, this path is not located inside a gated community, reserved for only a select few. Anyone who desires it can walk this path with God.

---

3. F. Brown, S. Driver, and C. Briggs, *The Brown-Driver-Briggs Hebrew and English Lexicon*, Unabridged, Electronic Database. 2002, 2003, 2006 by Biblesoft, Inc.

4. Zodhiates, *The Complete Word Study Dictionary New Testament*, 156.

5. Ibid., 156.

Additionally, there is more than one way to walk this ancient path. Spiritual journeying with Christ is not a pre-programmed, cookie-cutter affair. Rather, God works uniquely in each of our lives and makes use of our unique and varied personalities, preferences, and skill. In his classic book, *The Practice of the Presence of God*, Brother Lawrence experienced the presence of God just as strongly while doing mundane kitchen work in his monastery as during more seemingly spiritual settings such as times of Bible reading or formal worship and prayer.[6] For Lawrence, there was no distinction between secular and sacred, and he even offered up prayers addressed to the "Lord of all pots and pans."[7] The key to Lawrence's profound experience with the person and presence of Jesus Christ was to "recognize God intimately present with us, to address ourselves to Him every moment."[8]

Similarly to Lawrence, sixteenth century French mystic, Jeanne Guyon called followers of Jesus Christ into an interactive relationship with God through a contemplative approach to spirituality wherein the voice of God gets discerned and embraced on an internal, meditative level. In her work, *Experiencing the Depths of Jesus Christ*, she taught adherents how to withdraw from distractions and "keep turning within to the Lord's presence."[9] Contemporary authors such as Richard Foster, the late Dallas Willard, and Adele Ahlberg Calhoun have continued the discussion, expounding on additional spiritual practices that enable us to walk the ancient pathways with Jesus.[10]

For me, there have been several practices that have helped me walk the ancient path and stay healthy in my soul, despite some really terrible external circumstances. I would like to list a few of

---

6. Lawrence, *The Practice of the Presence of God*, 2.
7. Ibid., 11.
8. Ibid., 25.
9. Guyon, *Experiencing the Depths of Jesus Christ*, 25.
10. See Foster, *The Celebration of Discipline: The Path to Spiritual Growth*; Willard, *The Spirit of the Disciplines: Understanding How God Changes Lives*; and Calhoun, *Spiritual Disciplines Handbook: Practices That Transform Us*.

the practices here to help you start considering those that will best help *you* stay on this path as well.

Heritage

My parents became Christians when I was two, and I prayed to receive Jesus and follow Him when I was about five. I have been a Christian for forty years, and I have been walking with God in a focused, intentional relationship for over twenty-five years. Jessica and I have been married for twenty-three years; I have been in church ministry for twenty-one years, and I have been an ordained pastor for eighteen years. Throughout these years of faith, Jessica and I have often gotten exhausted in our souls. We have seen the ugly side of church work, the side that makes non-Christians want to steer clear of organized religion, and we have seen the ugly side of our own personal issues and failures as well. We have been disillusioned and distraught and we have often wanted to run. Conversely, we have also seen the church at its best. We have seen people respond to God's grace in its various forms. We have seen countless acts of God-inspired sacrificial love. Ultimately, we have seen Jesus, and that has made all the difference. We have become who we are today by keeping company with Jesus on the ancient path.

One of our favorite preachers in the early years of our marriage was an elderly gentleman named Dr. Syvelle Phillips, and we frequently heard him say, "I have seen enough in the church to make me an infidel." Then he would quickly add, "But I still have a made-up mind and a determination to see what lies at the end of a successful Christian race." Journeying on the ancient path has kept that same passion alive in Jessica and me as well. We are still in love with Jesus; we are still desperate to know Him better, and after all these years we feel as if we are just getting started in this amazing life of faith.

We have had our Jeremiah moments where we were angry and ready to quit, and we have also had our souls re-inflated along the way. For me personally, there have been five things that have made all the difference in my life. Whether you are new to Christianity, or have been following Jesus for many years, these can break you out of ruts or plateaus, and they can reorient your entire inner life. They are:

1. The voice of God.
2. The presence of God.
3. The Word of God.
4. The people of God.
5. And a life-long commitment to repentance.

The Voice of God

My entire spiritual life and development can be found inside the pages of a couple dozen leather journals. They are not terribly impressive. If you peeked inside them, you would not be moved or awed. If I died and my kids read my journals, they might be intrigued for a few pages, but would probably quickly move on. They are not profound and beautifully written. Nor are they packed with family memories like, "Dear Diary, today Amber and Maddie went to the beach." My journals are not autobiographical stories of my life, rather, they are records of the insights, struggles, processing, and affirmations that have come to me from God. They are the record of twenty-five years of trying to walk with God. They are tear-stained. Once, I even dropped my journal in a hot tub (word of wisdom: don't use a hair dryer on wet journal pages—it turns them brittle).

I don't write daily—probably just three or four times per week—and what I typically write are simple insights from my daily Bible reading. I write down interesting thoughts, prayers, or words that I believe might be direct communications from God. In church, we always tell people that prayer is conversation with God, but we don't always urge people to take time to listen, and this is unfortunate because a one-sided conversation is not really a conversation; it is a monologue. So, rather than merely practicing monologue prayers, I use my journal as a space to practice listening. Occasionally, I will write out a question for God, and then I will pause and listen to see if a response stirs in my soul. Sometimes, those moments are powerful; sometimes they aren't. Over the years though, my practicing of journaling and listening has built a steadily increasing sense of destiny and God's love in me.

Throughout the years, God has repeatedly affirmed and reaffirmed my calling. He has brought healing to my soul, and He has done all of the things that His word promises to do in Psalm 29. In Psalm 29, we are told that the voice of God breaks the cedars, shakes the deserts, and causes new life to emerge. Those things happen when we wait on God in prayer. A word from God is far more powerful than any human exhortation, and everything changes when we receive one. There is a vast difference between hearing a person say, "God loves you" and sensing God Himself whisper to our soul, "Child, I love you. You are mine." When God speaks, strongholds break, deserts blossom, and barrenness gives way to life.

For me, I have gotten literal with the idea of walking an ancient path. I love to walk during my prayer times, so throughout the years, I have walked dozens and dozens of miles in company with God, practicing the disciplines of prayer and listening, learning to perceive His presence.

The Presence of God

The presence of God is more than the warm, emotional *feelings* that accompany God's nearness, although it includes that. The presence of God is the reality of the active work of the Holy Spirit in a person's life.

I grew up in churches that believed in the Holy Spirit and talked about the gifts and activities of the Spirit, but in practice and experience I was often like the believers in Ephesus who said to the Apostle Paul, "We have not even heard that there is a Holy Spirit" (Acts 19:2). However, when I began responding to God's stirring work in my heart, I started intentionally reading about the Holy Spirit in Scripture, and I saw that there are three specific movements of Holy Spirit infilling.

The first occurs at conversion. When we believe in Jesus Christ and invite Him into our lives, we receive an infilling of the Holy Spirit. In John 20:22, Jesus breathed on His disciples and said, "Receive the Holy Spirit." Although the disciples were already followers of Jesus of course, this was their first opportunity to believe in Him after His resurrection from the dead. When He rose from the dead and breathed on His disciples, they received the Holy Spirit.

Subsequent to that conversion moment, however, there was another infilling. Even though Jesus had just breathed on His disciples and filled them with the life and Spirit of God, He instructed them to wait for another infilling. That second infilling, or empowerment, occurred on the day of Pentecost:

> When the day of Pentecost came they were all together in one place. Suddenly a sound like the blowing of a violent wind came from heaven and filled the whole house where they were sitting. They saw what seemed to be tongues of fire that separated and came to rest on each of them. All of them were filled with the Holy Spirit and began to speak in other tongues as the Spirit enabled them. (Acts 2:1-4).

In accordance with this passage, I began to pray, "Lord, if there is more for me to experience of your Holy Spirit, let me have it!" I spent many days, weeks even, specifically praying about this. One particular week I spent every lunch hour in the chapel of a local college asking God to give me more of the Spirit. That searching time of my life resulted in some powerful encounters with God that have stayed with me throughout my life.

The third infilling of the Holy Spirit, subsequent to conversion and additional infillings, is supposed to happen *today*. In Ephesians 5:18, the Apostle Paul said, "Do not get drunk on wine, which leads to debauchery. Instead, be filled with the Spirit." The comparison between alcohol and the Spirit is fascinating because

The Ancient Path

apparently the joy, freedom, and ability to loosen up that can happen with alcohol imbibing is something that can be eclipsed by an infilling of the Holy Spirit and a sense of God's nearness.

Additionally, the verb tense in this passage is significant. In Greek, the phrase "be filled" is a present imperative tense that means we are to seek an ongoing, present-day, real time infilling of the Spirit of God.[11] It is something that can happen *today*. Then, when today ends and tomorrow begins, we are to seek and experience it all over again.

Church debates surrounding the time, place, and nature of the baptism of the Holy Spirit are never-ending, and eminent scholars and theologians take up differing positions and perspectives. John R. W. Stott disagrees that there are multiple levels of Holy Spirit baptism or infilling, asserting, rather, that the baptism of the Holy Spirit is something that is "received once for all at conversion." Additionally, he states that the life and fullness of the Spirit is something that is "to be continuously and increasingly appropriated."[12] For Stott, "The baptism of the Spirit is not a second and subsequent experience enjoyed by some Christians, but the initial experience enjoyed by all."[13] Other scholars, such as Gordon D. Fee, hold different views. In his book, *Paul, the Spirit, and the People of God*, Fee concludes, "A substantial tradition in the church believes that such an experience of the Spirit, a 'baptism in the Spirit' if you will, is available to believers *subsequent* to their reception of the Spirit in conversion."[14]

Regardless of where one lands in the theological debate, the issue is not primarily whether we received the Spirit at conversion or in a post-conversion moment, but whether or not we have the life of the Spirit in us *today*. Everything changes when we are infused with God's Spirit, and according to the Apostle Paul, this is available today. A plain text reading of Scripture tells us that, yes, we receive the Holy Spirit at conversion, and yes, there is a

---

11. Zodhiates, *The Complete Word Study New Testament*, 641, 891.
12. Stott, *Baptism & Fullness: The Work of the Holy Spirit Today*, 63.
13. Ibid., 39.
14. Fee, *Paul, the Spirit, and the People of God*, 194.

post-conversion baptism of the Holy Spirit, but there is something even beyond that—*today*, be filled with the Spirit.

The Scriptures

I once heard Pastor Jack Hayford encourage a roomful of young pastors, "If you begin reading through the entire Bible every year when you are twenty, by the time you are forty it will pour out of you." This is true. In my early twenties, I was mentored in the skill of Bible reading, and I began following an annual Bible reading schedule that takes the reader through the Old Testament once and the New Testament, Psalms, and Proverbs twice each year. A pre-set Bible reading schedule is of inestimable value because it forces the reader to visit passages of Scripture that might normally get overlooked or bypassed, and it helps one see that the Scriptures are indeed a living document; whether we are reading in Genesis, Psalms, Mark, or Revelation, life and inspiration flows from the pages as we read. Additionally, a broad, frequent reading of Scripture enhances overall Bible understanding and preaching ability. Probably eighty-five percent of every sermon I have ever preached has come from my assigned Bible reading passages and my times of journaling.

Bible Study

It is worth noticing that the Scriptures admonish us to do more than merely read the Bible. Frequently, we are told to meditate on Scripture (Psalm 1:1–3; Psalm 119:15–16; Joshua 1:8) and study Scripture (Acts 17:11; 2 Timothy 2:15). In Deuteronomy 6:6–8 Moses urged the people to put the commandments on their hearts. Furthermore, he said, "Impress them on your children. Talk about them when you sit at home and when you walk along the road, and when you lie down and when you get up. Tie them as symbols on your hands and bind them on your foreheads. Write them on the doorframes of your houses and your gates." All of this imagery calls us to do more than merely read the Bible, but rather to absorb its content into every aspect of our lives.

In Jesus' famous walk down the road to Emmaus, He explained the Scriptures to two of His heart-broken disciples and they responded this way: "Were not our hearts burning within us while He talked with us on the road and opened the Scriptures to us?"[15] When the Scriptures are opened, light shines and hearts begin to burn.

Psalm 119:130 says, "The unfolding of your Word gives light," and when we move beyond a devotional reading of Scripture to a deeper, more studious examination of it, we experience that unfolding of light. Following cross references, perusing the textual notes and commentaries in our study Bibles, and even scouring Hebrew and Greek dictionaries for broader understanding all serve to enhance our experience with both the Scriptures themselves and the God that the Scriptures reveal.

The People of God

In a 1676 letter to his rival, Robert Hooke, Sir Isaac Newton expressed, "If I have seen a little further it is by standing on the shoulders of giants." This sentiment was likely a re-phrasing of a 12th century quote from author and theologian John of Salisbury: "We are like dwarfs sitting on the shoulders of giants. We see more, and things that are more distant, than they did, not because our sight is superior or because we are taller than they, but because they raise us up, and by their great stature add to ours."[16] Certainly, in the Christian life of faith, this sentiment is true. Although each of us must respond to Jesus individually, ours is not an individualistic faith; each of us must walk in the company of others, and each of us will have times when we can identify with the unnamed man

---

15. See Luke 24:32

16. P.J. Didapper, "Standing on the shoulders of giants," *The Pharmaceutical Journal Blog*, September 8, 2011, accessed January 20, 2018, https://www.pharmaceutical-journal.com/opinion/blogs/standing-on-the-shoulders-of-giants/11083715.

from the Gospels who lay stricken on a stretcher while four stout friends carried him to Jesus (Mark 2:1–12).

Once, after the death of our daughter, Alexis Grace, a pastor told me, "Sometimes just staying in the lifeboat is overcoming." I think he was right. Sometimes, just staying in the lifeboat while others do some of the heavier lifting for us is a stalwart, victorious act. Throughout my life, many noble people have walked beside me, sometimes supporting me and sometimes carrying me when I could not go on. From Jessica to family members to mentors and friends, the people of God have sustained me. I might have abandoned the ancient path if it were not for them, and their work in my life now inspires me to take my own turn at carrying others (incidentally, that too is a part of the ancient path).

A Life-long Commitment to Repentance

One of the greatest mentors in my life was Jessica's father, John Beal, and once when he was creating a blog post he described himself this way: "I am John Beal, the quester. . .and repentance is my best friend." When I first read his sentiment, I found it a bit archaic and un-relatable, but the more I pondered it, the more I saw the depth and wisdom that he was communicating. We, too, are on a quest, and when we, too, embrace a lifestyle of repentance, being quick to *shuwb*/return to the Lord, life becomes sweeter, richer, and vastly more satisfying.

Walking on Jeremiah's ancient path is quite different from merely attending church or casually joining a faith group. It is like moving from a long-distance relationship sustained by occasional letters and phone calls to a vibrant, daily relationship in personal time and space. It is the "tasting and seeing" that God is good,[17] and it has been the testimony of Christ followers all throughout church history that this path is indeed the way to a dynamic, towering, soul-restoring life.

Dynamic lives:

17. See Psalm 34:8

The Ancient Path

1. Run in a faster heat.
2. Are fueled and sustained by a word from God.
3. Stretch back farther than their family of origin and connect to the "before" of God.
4. Are quick to *shuwb*/return.
5. Carry a prophetic word from the Lord for others.
6. Are carriers of hope and proclaimers of judgment—they remind people that spring is coming, and they constantly call people back to their place in God.
7. Walk the ancient path in company with Jesus Christ.

Questions for Discussion

- How tired is your soul today?
- What kinds of activities help you rest and recover on the inside?
- Are you currently engaging in those activities, or do you need to make time to do them?
- What spiritual practices have helped you walk Jeremiah's ancient path?

CHAPTER 8

The Dread Champion

"But the LORD is with me, like a dread champion." (Jeremiah 20:11, NASB)

HAVE YOU EVER PURSUED a task, an errand, or a goal and had things *not* turn out the way you planned? Have you ever had dreams that never came about or great expectations that were dashed along the way? Did you ever hope for a new season of life, but when it finally arrived it was really just more of the same?

Some students dream that their high school years will be better than their junior high years, but they are not. Some college graduates anxiously await their first career level job, and then hate it when it arrives. Some people have fairy tale expectations for a first date experience, until the date turns awkward or disappointing.

I read an insightful book several years ago that urged people to write their entire life story in six succinct words. It is a powerful exercise, and sometimes the results can be quite funny: Never really finished anything besides cake. Sometimes they can be ironic: Bad brakes discovered at high speed. Sometimes they can be poignant and sad: I still make coffee for two. A dear friend of mine summarized his life story in these six profound words: Needed, found, became a safe place. The title of the book captured the deep disappointment that often accompanies our human experience: *Not Quite What I Was Planning*.[1]

For many of us, the title of the books says it all—our lives have not turned out exactly the way we planned. If you can relate to this sentiment, it does not mean that you are a gloomy Eeyore or that you don't have faith in God; it simply means that you are human, you are a flesh and blood human being living life on planet earth. It also means that you can relate to a significant portion of Jeremiah's life. Remember with me that Jeremiah's towering, dynamic life was lived in the middle of personal, relational, religious, and national conflict and controversy.

Remember how his story began. "The word of the LORD came to him in the thirteenth year of the reign of Josiah son of Amon king of Judah, and through the reign of Jehoiakim son of Josiah king of Judah, down to the fifth month of the eleventh year of Zedekiah son of Josiah king of Judah, when the people of Jerusalem went into exile" (Jeremiah 1:2–3).

As we saw earlier, Jeremiah lived during the final forty years of Israel's monarchy, and God called him into the role and office of a prophet at the exact same time that God was raising up another young man, king Josiah. Josiah was a boy king who ascended the throne after his father's assassination. Josiah's dad, Amon, was so worthless and evil that his own officials conspired to kill him, and at the time of his death the nation was teetering on the brink of collapse. Spiritually, Israel was nearly apostate. The people had generally walked away from God and embraced alternate religions and ideologies. And politically and economically, it was at risk of takeover from foreign governments. As God always did in times like that, He raised up leaders to announce His words and respond to the critical state of the nation. In this instance, He raised up two young people—a prophet and a king—to bring reform.

Josiah was one of the greatest kings that Israel ever had. Again, the Bible says this about his story:

---

1. Fershleiser, and Smith, ed., *Not Quite What I Was Planning: Six-Word Memoirs by Writers Famous and Obscure*.

Dynamic Living in Desperate Times

Josiah was eight years old when he became king, and he reigned in Jerusalem thirty-one years. He did what was right in the eyes of the LORD and followed the ways of his father David, not turning aside to the right or to the left. In the eighth year of his reign, while he was still young, he began to seek the God of his father David. In his twelfth year he began to purge Judah and Jerusalem of high places, Asherah poles and idols (2 Chronicles 34:1–3).

Later on, in the eighteenth year of Josiah's reign, he commissioned the rebuilding and restoration of the temple, and he reinstated true worship in the nation. He was a remarkable king. In fact, his story always reminds me of a humorous tough guy movie quote: "I've come to chew bubble gum and kick ass—and I'm all out of bubble gum."[2]

Josiah kicked butt and took names. He drove idol worship out of the country, he revived the priesthood, he renovated the Temple, and he called the nation to repent and return to the Lord. Can you imagine what would happen if the president of the United States did the same? Can you imagine a press conference where a sitting president might say, "Today, I would like to publicly repent for every arrogant, unclean, and inappropriate statement or action I have ever said or done"? And what if he continued, "Additionally, I would like to call our entire country to repent for every sinful act we have ever committed as a nation; I would like each of us to renounce the sins of racism, sexism, classism, ageism, and pride. As a country, let's return to God, embracing humility, worship, and obedience." King Josiah actually did that, and the whole nation responded.

In the early years of his ministry, Jeremiah supported Josiah, prophetically reinforcing the king's message. They were two young reformers—prophet and king—working together to call God's people back to their rightful place, and for several years it appeared to be working. The nation responded, worship and spirituality

---

2. *They Live*. DVD. Directed by John Carpenter. Los Angeles: Alive Films Larry Franco Productions, 1988.

surged, and Jeremiah likely thought, "Being God's prophet is not a bad gig." He preached; he prophesied; and the people responded—it was pretty much everything a prophet of God could hope for.

Unfortunately, things changed as they so often do. Josiah died in battle at just thirty-nine years old, and almost immediately after his death, the nation went back to its old ways. Apparently, Josiah's reforms were only skin-deep, and the nation regressed even further than it was before.

Josiah died without ever witnessing Israel's backsliding and relapse, but Jeremiah on the other hand lived for another twenty-two years, watching Israel move further and further away from God until they eventually disintegrated and went into captivity in Babylon. Listen to some of God's words to the young prophet at the end of Jeremiah's opening chapter:

> Get yourself ready! Stand up and say to them whatever I command you. Do not be terrified by them, or I will terrify you before them. Today I have made you a fortified city, an iron pillar and a bronze wall to stand against the whole land—against the kings of Judah, its officials, its priests and the people of the land. They will fight against you but will not overcome you, for I am with you and will rescue you, declares the LORD (Jeremiah 1:17-19).

That was not a very promising job description. How would you like God to say that to you? "Child, I am going to have to make you as strong as a bronze wall because these people are going to beat against you your entire ministry." Even though God promised to stand with Jeremiah amidst all of the conflict, this was still a daunting, overwhelming calling, and ultimately it happened exactly as God predicted. People fought against Jeremiah every day of his life, and he was almost always the odd man out.

Outcast

There was a group of prophets that continually told the reigning Israeli kings that God was pleased with the country and that Israel would be blessed. Jeremiah, however, was the lone, annoying naysayer. The prophets would say things like, "Oh king, God will certainly deliver us," and Jeremiah would always counter, "No, He won't."

When the popular prophetic voices predicted favor and prosperity, Jeremiah preached messages about repentance and lament. When the majority prophesied victory in battle, Jeremiah warned of impending doom unless the people returned to the Lord. Throughout the years, Jeremiah was mocked, ostracized, slapped, and imprisoned for his messages, as the nation steadily slipped further and further away from God.

At one point, the state of the nation became so perilous that God actually told Jeremiah not to marry. In Jeremiah 16:1–2, Jeremiah said, "Then word of the LORD came to me: 'You must not marry and have sons or daughters in this place.'" Sometimes, I hear people lament the tumultuous state of our world, and they make comments like, "I'm not sure if I would want to bring children into a world like ours today." God Himself said that same thing to Jeremiah in his day.

Jeremiah preached and pleaded and begged the people to respond to God. He was a dramatic, engaging prophet who often employed creative prophetic acts to better illustrate his messages, but the people never listened. Following Josiah's death and continuing through the reigns of the four weak and wicked kings who succeeded him, the people refused to respond to Jeremiah's message. Eventually, the nation of Egypt defeated Israel and deposed Israel's king, setting up a puppet monarch in his place. Some years after that, King Nebuchadnezzar from Babylon marched on Jerusalem, inflicting its ultimate defeat and initiating the infamous Babylonian exile.

As King Nebuchadnezzar's armies surrounded the city, all of the popular prophets began saying, "We have to fight. God will deliver us!" Meanwhile, Jeremiah said (you guessed it), "No, God is not with us. Nebuchadnezzar is going to win. In fact, the Lord wants us to submit to Nebuchadnezzar and go willingly into exile." It was not a popular message, but he was right.[3]

---

3. See Jeremiah 38:17–18

Jeremiah was never a popular figure, but he did develop a far-reaching reputation, and when King Nebuchadnezzar finally conquered Jerusalem it says this in Jeremiah 39:11–14:

> Now Nebuchadnezzar king of Babylon had given these orders about Jeremiah through Nebuzaradan commander of the imperial guard: "Take him and look after him; don't harm him but do for him whatever he asks." So Nebuzaradan...sent and had Jeremiah taken out of the courtyard of the guard. They turned him over to Gedaliah son of Ahikam, the son of Shaphan, to take him back to his home. So he remained among his own people.

The captain of the guard ultimately said to Jeremiah, "Today I am freeing you from the chains on your wrists. Come with me to Babylon, if you like, and I will look after you; but if you do not want to, then don't come. Look, the whole country lies before you; go wherever you please" (Jeremiah 40:4). All of the rich, powerful, and influential people were being taken into exile, and the Babylonians offered to take Jeremiah as well, promising to provide for him if he wanted, but in Jeremiah 40:6 it says that Jeremiah "stayed with him among the people who were left in the land."

It was not an easy decision for Jeremiah to stay behind in Jerusalem because after the attack on the city, Jerusalem was demolished—the temple was destroyed, the major buildings were burned to the ground, the walls were broken down, the city gates were torn apart, all of the powerful people were gone, and only the poorest of the poor were left behind in the ruined city. When God called Jeremiah to be a "prophet to the nations" Jeremiah never would have imagined that he would oversee the utter collapse of King David's empire.

Depressed

Jeremiah was prone to bouts of deep depression and discouragement, and when we consider his story it makes sense. Listen to one of his famous interactions with God:

Dynamic Living in Desperate Times

> You deceived me, LORD, and I was deceived; you overpowered me and prevailed. I am ridiculed all day long; everyone mocks me. Whenever I speak, I cry out proclaiming violence and destruction. So the word of the LORD has brought me insult and reproach all day long. But if I say, "I will not mention His word or speak anymore in His name," His word is in my heart like a fire, a fire shut up in my bones. I am weary of holding it in; indeed, I cannot. I hear many whispering, "Terror on every side! Denounce him! Let's denounce him!" All my friends are waiting for me to slip, saying, "Perhaps he will be deceived; then we will prevail over him and take our revenge on him" (Jeremiah 20:7-10).

How does somebody in that state live a dynamic life? How could Eugene Peterson call someone like that a "towering life, terrifically lived"?[4] When people were trying to figure out who Jesus Christ was, why would they think of a discouraged, defeated prophet like Jeremiah? How could a person like that stand so tall and powerful and compellingly in the middle of such shattered times?

I am not sure how much of Jeremiah's story we can actually relate to because comparatively we live in a fairly comfortable time and place in world history. However, if we had lived in London during the Nazi bombing blitz in World War II or in South Africa during its apartheid, we could have related. The people who lived in America during the Great Depression might have felt a little bit of what Jeremiah did, and so can the people today who live in high poverty, human trafficking conditions. But, regardless of the comparative depths of our pain, life seldom works out for us the way that we ultimately plan, and if any of us are going to live towering, terrific lives we will have to do it in the middle of tough times.

Fortunately, it can be done. Jeremiahs have always emerged in horrible times, and the next verse in Jeremiah's lament shows us how it happens. After complaining about being deceived and overpowered by God and insulted and attacked by people, Jeremiah

---

4. Peterson, *Run with The Horses*, 201.

says some of the most powerful words in all of Scripture. He says, "But the LORD is with me like a mighty warrior" (Jeremiah 20:11).
The Lord is with me, even when no one is listening to me.
The Lord is with me, even though King Josiah has died.
The Lord is with me, even when I am in prison and exile.
The Lord is with me, *like a mighty warrior.*

The NASB translation of the Bible renders the phrase this way: "The LORD is with me like a dread champion." Wow, what a statement!

Dread Champion

What is a dread champion? Quite simply, a dread champion is a champion that strikes dread in the hearts of an enemy army. Goliath was a dread champion. Do you remember what happened before David fought Goliath? In 1 Samuel 17:4, the Philistines were lined up against the Israelites for battle, and it says, "A champion named Goliath, who was from Gath, came out of the Philistine camp." The text then describes this fierce, nine-foot tall warrior and says, "On hearing the Philistine's words, Saul and all the Israelites were dismayed and terrified" (verse 11). Goliath was a "dread champion" (the Jerusalem Bible calls him a "shock trooper"), and his appearance and words filled Israel with dismay and terror.[5]

Somehow, Jeremiah was able to look up from his painful lot in life and say, "Despite everything that has gone wrong all around me despite all of the pain and disappointment and resistance in my world God is my Goliath! He is my shock soldier and my dread champion. He is my Mighty Warrior, and He will never fail me."

I love those humorous movie scenes where a bully or an enemy corners a weaker victim, and then suddenly their face assumes a terrified expression and they begin scrambling to run away. It is hilarious when the cornered individual begins to strut around and boast, "Yeah, that's right. You'd better run!" while failing to realize that a bigger, stronger ally has walked up behind them and scared

---

5. See: *The Jerusalem Bible* Reader's Edition, (Garden City, NY: Doubleday & Company, Inc., 1968).

their adversary away. The enemy was not running away from the cornered weakling, but from the dread champion behind them! God, our dread champion, is not a cosmic butler who will gift-wrap every one of our prayers and do everything exactly the way we were planning; however, He will sustain us. He will walk with us onto every battlefield of our life.

He will go with you into a new school year. He will go with you to college. He will walk beside you in your big job interview, and when you have children or grandchildren. He will walk as closely beside you in the painful, disappointed years, as He will in the glorious, golden ones. Jeremiah's dread champion walks beside you in your present moment, and He is prophesying a better future.

The Plans I Have for You

Jeremiah stayed behind in Jerusalem, preferring life among the poor to exile in Babylon, and from his place in the burned-out city he decided to write a letter to the Jewish exiles. Do you recognize this letter? Here is some of its content:

> This is the text of the letter that the prophet Jeremiah sent from Jerusalem to the surviving elders among the exiles and to the priests, the prophets and all the other people Nebuchadnezzar had carried into exile from Jerusalem to Babylon. This is what the LORD Almighty, the God of Israel, says to all those I carried into exile from Jerusalem to Babylon: "Build houses and settle down; plant gardens and eat what they produce. Marry and have sons and daughters; find wives for your sons and give your daughters in marriage, so that they too may have sons and daughters. Increase in number there; do not decrease. Also, seek the peace and prosperity of the city to which I have carried you into exile. Pray to the LORD for it, because if it prospers, you too will prosper." This is what the LORD says: "When seventy years are completed for Babylon, I will come to you and fulfill my good promise to bring you back to this place. For I know

the plans I have for you," declares the LORD, "plans to prosper you and not to harm you, plans to give you hope and a future" (Jeremiah 29:1, 4–7, 10–11).

Do you love Jeremiah 29:11? Everybody seems to love this verse. People even print it on bumper stickers and hang it on their cars. It was not written when everything was going great though. It was not a promise for an easy, simple life. It was written under the shadow of an oppressive enemy when everything seemed lost.

It was a promise that the story would not end there.

Seventy years later, Daniel, an old man in exile in Babylon, read Jeremiah's words, and he started doing a little math. He realized that the seventy years from Jeremiah's letter were expired, so he began praying and asking God for deliverance.[6] Then, right on schedule, Babylon got attacked and conquered by Cyrus the King of Persia, *and Cyrus set the exiles free.*[7]

From Exile to Jesus

Eventually, the exiles came home; the temple was rebuilt; an angel prophesied to a young virgin named Mary, and she gave birth to Jesus, the Savior of the world. Thirty years after His birth, when people were trying to figure out who He was, one of the most popular guesses was Jeremiah. Jeremiah's dread champion had won the day. Today, nearly three thousand years after Jeremiah watched his beloved people go into exile, we are still worshipping under the shadow of that same dread champion. His purposes have never been stopped, His kingdom will never fail to advance, and the plans He has for us are still good.

A dread champion is better than a cosmic butler. I cannot promise you that God will say yes to all of your prayers. I cannot guarantee you perfectly smooth sailing in every season of your life, but I can promise you that you will never sail alone. Jeremiah's

---

6. See Daniel 9:1–3
7. See 2 Chronicles 36:20–23

dread champion walks beside you, and your future is vastly more significant than you could ever imagine.

One of my pastor friends reports an interesting phenomenon that often occurs when he prays. When he senses God's presence or voice, he perceives the presence of a great lion standing behind him and looking over his shoulder. I don't know if my friend has read *The Chronicles of Narnia* too many times and he is projecting C.S. Lewis' Aslan character into his relationship with God, or maybe God likes to appear to my friend in His biblical role of "the Lion of the tribe of Judah" (Revelation 5:5). Regardless, it is good imagery. The Lion of the tribe of Judah, the dread champion, Jesus Christ is with *you*, and His promise from Hebrews 13:5-6 still stands: "God has said, 'Never will I leave you; never will I forsake you.' So we say with confidence, 'The LORD is my helper; I will not be afraid. What can mere mortals do to me?'"

Dynamic lives:

1. Run in a faster heat.
2. Are fueled and sustained by a word from God.
3. Stretch back farther than their family of origin and connect to the "before" of God.
4. Are quick to *shuwb*/return.
5. Carry a prophetic word from the Lord for others.
6. Are carriers of hope and proclaimers of judgment—they remind people that spring is coming, and they constantly call people back to their place in God.
7. Walk the ancient path in company with Jesus Christ.
8. Rest beneath the shadow of the dread champion.

Questions for Discussion

- Can you relate with the book title, *Not Quite What I Was Planning*?
- Where has life disappointed you? Where has it exceeded your expectations?

- Where do you need to see the presence of the dread champion in your life?
- Do you believe that God's plans for you are still good?

CHAPTER 9

The Potter's House

"This is the word that came to Jeremiah from the LORD: 'Go down to the potter's house, and there I will give you my message.'" (Jeremiah 18:1–2)

HAVE YOU EVER GONE on a field trip with God? It was probably a fun moment for Jeremiah when he unexpectedly heard God say, "Hey, son, let's mix it up today. Let's go on a field trip to the Potter's house. By the way, be sure to bring your journal because I am going to speak to you while we are there."

Sure enough, when Jeremiah arrived at the pottery shop, the Lord began to speak, and Jeremiah started writing things down, "So I went down to the potter's house, and I saw him working at the wheel. But the pot he was shaping from the clay was marred in his hands; so the potter formed it into another pot, shaping it as seemed best to him" (Jeremiah 18:3–4).

Don't you love the nonchalance in Jeremiah's tone? He said essentially, "The pot was ruined. . .so the potter re-made it." There was no stress or anxiety in Jeremiah's observation. He didn't panic when he saw how damaged the vessel was, and he didn't cry out, "Oh no, what are we going to do?" I like that, because sometimes you and I are like the damaged clay. Sometimes, we sin or make foolish decisions that hurt us and twist us into different shapes from what God intended for our lives, and we need the potter to put us back together again, too.

The pot was ruined, *so the potter formed it into another pot, as seemed best to him.* Isn't that beautiful? Even our worst decisions cannot take us beyond the power of God's grace to reach us and re-make us amid our failures and regrets.

No matter where you have been, no matter what you have done, and no matter what you have lost along the way, the Master Potter can still shape you into a vessel of honor "holy, useful to the Master and prepared to do any good work" (2 Timothy 2:21). The simple key to this re-shaping is to *respond*.

The Potter's Touch

I once heard the story of a man who asked an Irish potter why some of the vessels in her pottery shop were so beautiful and elegant while others were more misshapen and marred. He asked the potter, "Were you trying to make different kinds of vessels when you made the beautiful ones and the damaged ones?"

The potter replied, "No, I always try to produce beautiful, elegant vessels."

"Then what was the difference?" the customer asked. "Did you use different clay for the different vessels?"

Again the potter replied, "No, I took the clay for each vessel from the same source of clay."

The man persisted, "Then did you use a different shaping process when you made them?"

The potter shook her head, "No. I shaped each of them in the exact same process I always use."

Then an idea dawned and the customer asked, "Did you leave the damaged vessel in the fire too long? Perhaps that is why one of the vessels emerged damaged and the other did not."

Once more, the potter shook her head, "No."

"Then what was the difference?" the baffled man exclaimed. "Why would two pieces of clay taken from the same source, shaped exactly the same way, and fired for the same length of time end up completely different?"

The potter paused thoughtfully and then answered. "I am not sure if you can understand this without being a potter yourself, but the best way that I can answer your question is to say this: this beautiful vessel responded to my touch, whereas this damaged one did not."

The key to dynamic living in desperate times is to constantly respond to the master potter's touch, and the first way to respond is to always say, "yes." In our personal, internal responses to God, let's set our default response to "yes." Let's never lose our "yes." Let's forever pray: "God use me where I'm needed most," and then when God makes it clear where that is, let's respond by saying, "yes."

Pulling the Clay Up

I learned something about pottery a few years ago that makes it easier to say yes. When a potter shapes a vessel she or he only pulls the clay *up;* they never push it *down.* In fact, the technical term for shaping or molding clay is "pulling the clay."[1] A master potter pulls the clay *up* into its destined shape; they never smash it down. And that principle carries over to people as well. People grow best when they are pulled up, loved, inspired, and believed in. In Psalm 18:35, King David said to God, "Your gentleness makes me great" (NASB).

Who Are You Pulling Up?

Dynamic living after the order of Jeremiah necessitates serving, pulling others *up*. It is impossible to live dynamically if one is living only to please oneself. Jesus' words still echo through time and space: "Whoever wants to save their life will lose it, but whoever

---

1. Bill Geisinger, "Basic Throwing," *Ceramicsweb.org*, accessed January 29, 2018, http://ceramicsweb.org/articles/tech_handouts/basic_throwing.html.

loses their life for me will find it."[2] Who are you losing your life for? To whom are you giving it? There are three areas of responsibility to which we should give our lives: the people in our measure, the people we encounter, and causes that transcend our reach.

First, the people in our measure. In 2 Corinthians 10:13, the Apostle Paul said that he refused to boast beyond the measure, or the sphere of influence, that God had assigned to him. We all have a measure. We all have a metered off space of influence containing people for whom we are responsible. Those particular people are our first priority. When someone in our measure needs lifting, we must be the first ones in line to pick them up.

Next, are the people we encounter. Although we cannot solve all of the world's problems, we can certainly bring some assistance or succor to the problems that strategically present themselves to us throughout our daily lives. Dynamic lives are available lives that are willing to see, stop, and pull someone *up*.

Finally, it is beneficial to the soul and essential for the world for us to find and serve a cause that transcends our personal reach. Perhaps it is something like the abolition of modern slavery or sex trafficking. My congregation, Grace Church of La Verne, recently fell in love with a couple named Don and Bridget Brewster who moved their home to a tiny village in Cambodia and established a ministry called Agape International Missions, where they are engaged in the fight to abolish sex trafficking in Cambodia and the world.

Their town is situated directly outside Cambodia's capitol city, Phnom Penh, and it was formerly a breeding ground for the sex trafficking epidemic. Tragically, in its history, the vast majority of young women in the village had been used for commercialized sex. Not only did Don and Bridget move their ministry into that place, but they eventually purchased a former brothel where underage girls had routinely been sold, and they turned it into their ministry headquarters. In the recesses of the brothel was a space called "the pink room" wherein the youngest girls were sold and abused. Today, the former pink room is now a headquarters for

2. Matthew 16:25

abolition, justice, healing, and change![3] At the time of this writing, Agape International Missions (AIM) has rescued one thousand children, women, and men from the sex trafficking industry and seen over eight hundred of them restored and reintegrated into society.[4]

Whether it is anti-trafficking, poverty relief, educational reform, church planting, or something else, find a cause that is bigger than your reach. Give to it. Pray for it. Support it. Doing so will bless the world while also expanding and increasing the life inside your soul.

When Jeremiah noticed how the potter re-shaped the damaged vessel, God spoke to his heart. "Then the word of the LORD came to me. He said, 'Can I not do with you, Israel, as this potter does?' declares the LORD. 'Like clay in the hand of the potter, so are you in my hand, Israel'" (Jeremiah 18:5–6). It is impossible to go through life unscathed. Some of our wounding will come from outside sources, and some will be self-inflicted when we make decisions that ultimately come back to hurt us. However, we can be confident that God is our master potter, and if we continue responding, forever saying yes to His touch while reaching out to pull other people *up*, He will shape us into worthy vessels that can be used for noble purposes in our world.

Dynamic lives:

1. Run in a faster heat.
2. Are fueled and sustained by a word from God.
3. Stretch back farther than their family of origin and connect to the "before" of God.
4. Are quick to *shuwb*/return.
5. Carry a prophetic word from the Lord for others.

---

3. *The Pink Room* documentary can be viewed at https://agapewebsite.org/pinkroom/

4. See: Agape International Missions. Accessed April 14, 2018. https://agapewebsite.org/

6. Are carriers of hope and proclaimers of judgment—they remind people that spring is coming, and they constantly call people back to their place in God.
7. Walk the ancient path in company with Jesus Christ.
8. Rest beneath the shadow of the dread champion.
9. Respond to the master potter's touch—and only pull people *up*.

Questions for Discussion

- In what areas of your life has God re-shaped you?
- Is it natural for you to pull others up or do you have to work at it?
- Who do you know that consistently pulls you up?
- Who in your life needs you to pull them up?

CHAPTER 10

Quicksand

"They lowered Jeremiah by ropes. . .and Jeremiah sank down into the mud." (Jeremiah 38:6)

HAVE YOU EVER BEEN stuck in quicksand? Have you ever seen actual quicksand? When my childhood best friend and I were about ten years old, we ran away from home for a few hours. We lived in the middle of national forests in the Pacific Northwest, and we both felt "the call of the wild." We had just finished reading Jack London's book, *The Call of the Wild*, and we felt like we were experiencing that same internal call and we had no choice but to leave civilization and head out into the wild on our own.[1]

In anticipation of our new life we filled our backpacks with canteens of water and packets of saltine crackers. We grabbed our pocketknives, we said goodbye to our little brothers, and we ran away. Our new life didn't last long (in fact, by the time my mom came home from work and my distraught little brother was telling her about our decision to leave, I was already walking back toward the house), but I vividly remember something about that day. My friend and I were terribly frightened by the prospect of two things: leeches and quicksand.

---

1. See: London, *The Call of the Wild*.

Quicksand

I had never seen a leech before, but our wilderness trek took us through several acres of swampy marshland, so we were constantly on the lookout for bloodsucking leeches that might attach to our ankles or calves. Additionally, we were afraid of falling into quicksand. At ten years old, we didn't realize that there are not any deadly quicksand pits in Pacific Northwest forests, so we prudently made a contingency plan in case we stumbled into some. We had wisely packed a length of rope in one of our backpacks, so when we approached a particularly murky section of swamp water we each tied an end of the rope around our waist so that if one of us fell into quicksand the other could hoist us out.

Fortunately, we were fine—the quicksand didn't get us—but we really did experience a legitimate fear. The fear of being buried alive is fairly common. I have watched people at the beach get horribly fidgety and nervous when a friend begins covering them in the sand, and that is when they are laying on top of the sand with just a thin layer of sand blanketing them. When a person begins sinking into literal quicksand, it can be terrifying, and Jeremiah knew about this terror firsthand.

When Jerusalem came under siege from the Babylonians, Jeremiah was arrested, due to his unrelenting prophetic messages. He knew that Israel was bound for exile, and he knew that resistance would be futile and would incur unnecessary damage, so he consistently pleaded with the king to submit to the Babylonian army and go peacefully into exile. In Jeremiah 38:2-3 he said:

> This is what the LORD says: "Whoever stays in this city will die by the sword, famine or plague, but whoever goes over to the Babylonians will live. They will escape with their lives; they will live." And this is what the LORD says: "This city will certainly be given into the hands of the army of the king of Babylon, who will capture it."

The king's officers and officials responded and said to the king, "This man should be put to death. He is discouraging the soldiers who are left in this city, as well as all the people, by the things he is saying to them. This man is not seeking the good of these people but their ruin" (Jeremiah 38:4).

It is certainly understandable that the officers would dislike Jeremiah's counsel. Their city was under siege, they could peer over the walls into the ranks of the enemy's army, and no good officer wants to hear a naysayer declaring that defeat is imminent. They hated Jeremiah's frequent admonition, "Sorry guys, it is time for exile. It is hopeless to resist. Submit and you'll be okay; resist, and you're toast."

Unfortunately, King Zedekiah agreed with his officers and said to them, "He is in your hands. The king can do nothing to oppose you" (Jeremiah 38:5).

King Zedekiah

Have you ever had a King Zedekiah in your life? Zedekiahs are tough to deal with because they are weak and wishy-washy, and you never quite know where you stand with them. Jeremiah interacted with multiple kings throughout his ministry. He was a friend to the good king Josiah; he was an enemy to the wicked King Jehoiakim (King Jehoiakim hated Jeremiah and constantly opposed him); but Zedekiah was hard to figure out. He always kept Jeremiah a little bit off balance. He legitimately liked Jeremiah, but he was quick to turn on him when their association became unpopular. He could be relationally hot then cold, and Jeremiah never knew exactly what his disposition would be.

Have you ever interacted with people like that? You think, "This person says that they like me, but I can tell that they don't." Or, "They keep telling me everything is okay, but I keep getting a vibe that it's not." Zedekiah was like that, and when his men demanded Jeremiah's punishment, he complied.

After telling his men that they could do whatever they desired with Jeremiah, the officers promptly "took Jeremiah and put him into the cistern of Malkijah, the king's son, which was in the courtyard of the guard. They lowered Jeremiah by ropes into the cistern; it had no water in it, only mud, and Jeremiah sank down into the mud" (Jeremiah 38:6).

Sinking in The Mud

Have you ever "sunk down into the mud" like Jeremiah did? Sinking into the mud is the opposite picture of the freedom that God wants to bring in people's lives. In the Old Testament there are two recurring pictures of what God's freedom looks like: it looks like *a firm foundation* and *room to run*.

In Psalm 40:2 David said, "He lifted me out of the slimy pit, out of the mud and mire; He set my feet on a rock and gave me a firm place to stand," and in Psalm 18:19, he said that God brought him into a "spacious place" where there was plenty of room to run.

A firm foundation and room to run—those evaporate when we start sinking into the mud. Most of us have never been swallowed up by literal quicksand, but probably all of us have had times when we felt like life was swallowing us up whole. As a child in pre-school, I learned a terrible song that said, "I'm being swallowed by a Boa Constrictor, and I don't like it very much." In those times when life is swallowing us alive, we feel some of the same things that a person feels when they are being swallowed up by literal quicksand, and we begin asking some of the same questions.

How Deep Does This Thing Go?

How low am I going to sink? How far underground is this sand going to pull me? We immediately think those things when life's quicksand pits begin pulling us down. A person might only be up to their ankles in financial quicksand, but when they feel the suction, they begin to fear, "Am I going all the way under?" Someone else might only be up to their knees in relational trauma, but they start thinking, "This is going to suffocate me. I'm not going to be able to breathe."

That is the nature of quicksand moments; they make us fear what *might* happen, not just what is actually happening. How far will I sink? How deep is this going to take me? If we are going to live dynamic, towering lives, we are going to have to live them in the middle of some quicksand seasons.

So how did Jeremiah do it? Since he is our model for dynamic living in desperate times, how did he pull himself up, and crawl out of his slimy, slippery pit?

The answer is *he didn't*.

There are times in our lives, no matter how daring or dynamic we aspire to be, when we cannot help ourselves. There are times when we sink too low and we become too stuck. Towering lives that are terrifically lived occasionally need rescuing. Have you experienced that? I have, and I hated it. I wish I could pass every test in life, overcome every obstacle, always stay strong, and win every round. But I can't. And neither could Jeremiah. And neither can you.

Ebed-Melek

In Jeremiah 38:7, a man named Ebed-Melek heard of Jeremiah's plight, and he petitioned King Zedekiah to set Jeremiah free. Although the king had just endorsed Jeremiah's imprisonment, his wishy-washy nature surfaced again, and he changed his mind. He now authorized Jeremiah's release, and Ebed-Melek set about rescuing the sinking prophet.

It is interesting to note that out of everyone in the palace, it was Ebed-Melek who wanted to set Jeremiah free. The text tells us that Ebed-Melek was an Ethiopian eunuch. He was from a minority culture, serving in the king's court in Israel, and at some point, in his life he had become castrated. Whether he was born a eunuch or had been painfully made one by a leader or oppressor, we can safely surmise that he had lived through his own seasons of pain.

It is hard to imagine a worse experience than castration. If you had been castrated, you would always be able to win the "who's having the worst day" game. If someone lamented their bad luck on a given day, you could always trump them with your own plight. "Oh, you're having a bad day? Well, I had my _____ cut off." Or, "I'm so sorry that life is a little bit stressful for you right now. But at least you still have your _____." I think it is remarkable that Ebed-Melek, out of everyone in the palace, was willing to reach out to someone else in pain.

Or maybe it wasn't that remarkable after all.

When I think about it, it seems perfectly logical that Ebed-Melek would be the one to help Jeremiah. People who have lived through the most pain are often the most concerned about other people's pain. As I professionally observe and interact with people, I notice that the people who have gone through significantly difficult times are rarely ever the ones who lack compassion. The people who lack compassion are the ones who really have not hurt that much.

When a person has sunk deeply into their own muddy cistern, they usually have empathy for other people's problems. They do not offer platitudes when someone else begins to sink. They do not give cheap, pat answers to the deep, troubling questions of life, and they don't get irritated when they are called upon to help. Instead, they go to the king. They begin to intercede.

Vessels of Mercy

One of my devotional books has a picture of a painting in it that shows two men grappling together on the edge of a cliff. At first glance, it appears that they are fighting each other, but after closer observation you realize that one man is actually trying to untangle the other man from a heavy burden on his back. Interestingly, the helping man has a burden strapped on his own shoulders too, and at the bottom of the picture there is a caption that reads: "Your own need for mercy has made you a vessel of mercy."[2]

I like Ebed-Melek. He was able to see beyond himself, and when the entire world around him got crazy (remember, Jerusalem was under siege and about to fall to the Babylonians) he still remembered a lone, individual *person* who was hurting. He heard Jeremiah crying, he found out about his condition, and he

---

2. Slagle, *From the Father's Heart: A Glimpse of God's Nature and Ways*, 65.

interceded with the king. Then he did something else that was remarkable. Look at how he went about rescuing Jeremiah:

> Ebed-Melek took the men with him and went to a room under the treasury in the palace. He took some old rags and worn-out clothes from there and let them down with ropes to Jeremiah in the cistern. Ebed-Melek the Cushite said to Jeremiah, "Put these old rags and worn-out clothes under your arms to pad the ropes." Jeremiah did so, and they pulled him up with the ropes and lifted him out of the cistern (Jeremiah 38:11–13).

Don't you love that? When Ebed-Melek rescued Jeremiah, he lowered padding for Jeremiah to put under his arms so the rescue ropes would not tear his skin. Sometimes a person's rescue efforts can actually damage the person that is being rescued. If we are not careful like Ebed-Melek was, we can sometimes hurt the very people we are trying to help. We need to be very gentle when we try to pull people out of their cisterns.

Sometimes we are not as gentle as we should be because we are so afraid of the mud. We are so worried about what is happening to a person that we pull too hard and end up dislocating their shoulder or tearing their skin in the process. Certainly, it would be better to suffer a dislocation than to suffocate to death in the mud, but if possible, let's be like Ebed-Melek and let's use enough gentleness and sensitivity to preserve the health of the people we are striving to pull back up to life.

Have You Ever Needed Rescuing?

Sometimes it is very humbling to need rescuing, isn't it? It can feel like failure to say, "I need help; I cannot do this on my own." However, it is not failure. It is actually Gospel. Jesus Christ drew near to us in our brokenness and lowered the padded ropes to us. Actually, that is not true. He did more than that. Jesus did not just lower some ropes into our pit; He actually jumped in after us, placed us on His shoulders, and began carrying us out.

Quicksand

There will be times in our lives when dynamic living requires humility. We will have to get over our pride and ask someone to help us. Sometimes, we will need prayer, encouragement, counsel, or medical attention, and in those moments, it won't be our pride that saves the day; it will be our humility, expressed as a plea for help. "Hey, I'm stuck, and I can't do this on my own. I made King Zedekiah mad, I got myself into a mess, life has swallowed me whole, and now I need your help."

Jeremiah probably did not look very heroic as he sagged weakly against the ropes while being drawn unceremoniously up out of the mud by his armpits. He probably was not a commanding, dynamic figure with his mud-stained, tear-streaked cheeks, and his gaunt, hunger-starved expression. You and I will not look very heroic either when we finally reach out for help, but that's okay; we actually will be. Everyone needs an Ebed-Melek in his or her corner, and sometimes it is a heroic act to reach out to him.

Additionally, part of the heroism that we are called to in our pursuit of dynamic living emerges when we become Ebed-Melek for someone else. We will never truly live a fully dynamic existence until *we* are Ebed-Melek and we spend some time rescuing sinking Jeremiahs.

Dynamic lives:

1. Run in a faster heat.
2. Are fueled and sustained by a word from God.
3. Stretch back farther than their family of origin and connect to the "before" of God.
4. Are quick to *shuwb*/return.
5. Carry a prophetic word from the Lord for others.
6. Are carriers of hope and proclaimers of judgment—they remind people that spring is coming, and they constantly call people back to their place in God.
7. Walk the ancient path in company with Jesus Christ.
8. Rest beneath the shadow of the dread champion.

9. Respond to the master potter's touch—and only pull people *up*.
10. Let others help them when they need it.

Questions for Discussion

- Is it difficult for you to ask for help?
- Are there any areas of your life where you should be asking for help, but aren't? If so, why aren't you?
- Have you ever hurt anyone in your attempts to help them? How could you have done it differently?
- Have you been Ebed-Melek in someone else's story?

CHAPTER 11

The Fire in Your Bones

"His word is in my heart like a fire, a fire shut up in my bones." (Jeremiah 20:9)

THE APOSTLE PAUL SAID, "Woe to me if I do not preach the Gospel."[1]

What is your "woe"? What is it that you are compelled to do? What fire is currently smoldering, shut up in your bones?

One of the most remarkable aspects of Jeremiah's life is that he never lost his passion; his flame never went out. Certainly, he had some touch-and-go moments where it looked like he might surrender. He faced enough opposition to make him doubt his calling at times. Once, late in his life when Jehoiakim was king, the Lord asked Jeremiah to gather all of the individual words that God had ever given him and assemble them into one comprehensive document. It was a daunting task, and yet he faithfully dictated every word from his entire ministry to his assistant, Baruch, who dutifully wrote them onto a massive scroll. Afterward, the scroll was presented to King Jehoiakim in the hope that he might respond to its words and lead the people into a humbler demeanor before God.[2]

---

1. See 1 Corinthians 9:16
2. See Jeremiah 36:1–4

Rather than responding in humility however, Jehoiakim made a mockery of Jeremiah's scroll. He asked a servant to read Jeremiah's words to him, and then while the servant read, the king leaned forward and systematically cut the scroll into tiny pieces, throwing each piece into a burning fireplace. Jeremiah 36:24 describes the king's defiance, "The king and all his attendants who heard all these words showed no fear, nor did they tear their clothes."

Opposition like that can make even the stoutest heart begin to doubt. When someone is so entrenched in their stubbornness and their refusal to respond to God, it can be easy for the prophet to despair. Before Jeremiah had time to run up a white surrender flag though, God spoke to him again. He said, "Take another scroll and write on it all the words that were on the first scroll, which Jehoiakim king of Judah burned up" (Jeremiah 36:28). So Jeremiah called Baruch, and they started the process all over again.

When someone has fire inside their bones, they can carry on even in the face of tremendous resistance or opposition. In his essay on Shattered Dreams, Dr. Martin Luther King Jr. wrote:

> At times in our lives the tail winds of joy, triumph, and fulfillment favor us, and at times the head winds of disappointment, sorrow, and tragedy beat unrelentingly against us. Our refusal to be stopped, our "courage to be," our determination to go on "in spite of," reveal the divine image within us. The man who has made this discovery knows that no burden can overwhelm him and no wind of adversity can blow his hope away. He can stand anything that can happen to him.[3]

In his classic work on *Spiritual Leadership*, J. Oswald Sanders wrote of the fire that burned in Count Nikolaus von Zinzendorf's heart for the cause of Christ, causing him to launch a world-changing missionary initiative: "His attitude toward ambition was summed up in one simple statement: 'I have one passion: it is He, He alone.'"[4] Zinzendorf's followers, the Moravians of the 1700s,

---

3. King, *Strength to Love*, 94.
4. Sanders, *Spiritual Leadership: Principles of Excellence for Every Believer*,

followed his lead, carrying a fire and passion for the cause of Jesus Christ into the nations of their day. Indeed, the fire in Count Zinzendorf's bones was so contagious that "one of every ninety-two Moravians left home to serve as a missionary."[5]

What is your "one passion"? What compels and motivates you to carry on even when circumstances are set against you? You probably don't have to think very hard to identify it—the presence of fire is readily apparent, warming us and illuminating us to our destiny.

When I Teach I Feel Like Me

The 2007 film, *Freedom Writers*, beautifully illustrates the power of fire in a person's bones. Hillary Swank stars as Erin Gruwell, a high school teacher for at risk students at Woodrow Wilson Classical High School in Long Beach, California, and all throughout the film her passion for her students is stunning. She combats racism, introduces them to the horrors of the Holocaust and the bravery of its survivors, and she works additional part-time jobs to buy special textbooks for her underprivileged students. At one point, her husband becomes frustrated with her sacrifice and commitment, and she explains simply, "When I teach I feel like me."[6]

When do you feel like *you*? What is it that best expresses the essence of who you are on the inside? Puritan church leader, Richard Baxter, once expressed his passion, "I preached as never sure to preach again, and as a dying man to dying men."[7] What cause or activity evokes that same passion in you? Are you artistic or analytical? Research-oriented or people-oriented? Do you have a passion for numbers or words or food? Does your heart ache for victims of human trafficking or for other kinds of victims who live

---

16.

5. Ibid., 16.

6. *Freedom Writers*. Film. Directed by Richard LaGravanese. Los Angeles, CA: MTV Films Jersey Films, 2007.

7. See: Beeke, and Pederson, *Meet the Puritans: With a Guide to Modern Reprints*.

in fancy homes in wealthy gated neighborhoods? God uniquely wired you for a cause. It was part of your "before," and when you identify it and embrace it the flame in your bones burns brighter. In *The Valley of Vision,* a Puritan prayer expresses this powerful sentiment, "There are two things worth living for: to further your cause in the world, and to do good to the souls and bodies of men; this is my ministry, my life, my prayer, my end. Grant me grace that I shall not fail."[8]

Fire Produces Faith

Dynamic living always requires an element of faith, and when one's heart is enflamed with passion for a great cause, it is much easier to maintain that faith. Near the end of Israel's independence, as the nation was about to capitulate to the Babylonians, the LORD asked Jeremiah to make the most remarkable, counter-intuitive, faith declaration. He asked him to purchase a piece of property along the doomed countryside. While everyone was scrambling to liquidate and prepare for the Babylonian invasion, God said, "Not you, Jeremiah. I want you to stand in faith."

Jeremiah's cousin owned a family field at Anathoth in the territory of Benjamin, and in the presence of the Jews who were gathered in the courtyard of the king's guard, Jeremiah purchased it. He purchased it with these words, "This is what the LORD Almighty, the God of Israel, says: 'Houses, fields and vineyards will again be bought in this land'" (Jeremiah 32:15). Eugene Peterson commented about Jeremiah's purchase of the land:

> It was crazy because at the very moment that he was buying it, the Babylonian armies were camping on it. The enemy was pounding the city walls and about to take the people off to exile. At that moment Jeremiah bought a field on which he would never plant an olive tree, prune a

---

8. Bennet ed., *The Valley of Vision: A Collection of Puritan Prayers & Devotions*, 343.

grapevine or build a house—a field that in all probability he would never even see.[9]

Why would God ask Jeremiah to do this? And how did Jeremiah have enough faith to comply?

Peterson continues, "The essential reality for Jeremiah was not that the Babylonians were camped on that field in Anathoth, but that God was using that ground to fulfill his promises. He bought the field as an investment in God's next project for Israel."[10] Ultimately, Jeremiah's purchase of the field at Anathoth was a deliberate act of faith-laced hope. The fire in his bones convinced him that the God who had called him from his youth was still at work, and that God's purposes would never be ultimately overthrown. When everyone else is selling their property and running away, dynamic lives say, "No, God is not finished with us yet. I am buying the field because I *know* that God will reverse our exile and eventually bring us back home." Dynamic lives believe God and fight endlessly for His cause.

Dynamic lives:

1. Run in a faster heat.
2. Are fueled and sustained by a word from God.
3. Stretch back farther than their family of origin and connect to the "before" of God.
4. Are quick to *shuwb*/return.
5. Carry a prophetic word from the Lord for others.
6. Are carriers of hope and proclaimers of judgment—they remind people that spring is coming, and they constantly call people back to their place in God.
7. Walk the ancient path in company with Jesus Christ.
8. Rest beneath the shadow of the dread champion.

---

9. Peterson, *Run with The Horses*, 169.
10. Ibid., 170.

Dynamic Living in Desperate Times

9. Respond to the master potter's touch—and only pull people *up*.
10. Let others help them when they need it.
11. Have a fire in their bones.

Questions for Discussion

- How is the fire in your bones—is it burning bright or does it need attention?
- How is your faith—if God calls you to buy a field near Anathoth are you ready to comply?
- Where are you excelling in your pursuit of dynamic living?
- Where do you need to be strengthened so you can grow?

CHAPTER 12

Your Context

"The word of the LORD came to him in the thirteenth year of the reign of Josiah..."
(Jeremiah 1:2)

SEVERAL YEARS AGO, I officiated the funeral for Don Paulson. He was not a celebrity or a public figure, and he was never externally successful as measured by many of today's standards. He was, however, a remarkable man. He died at ninety-five years old, and he spent the last seventy-five years of his life as a member of my congregation, Grace Church of La Verne. He was a modern-day shepherd (an interesting profession for someone living in Southern California), and even in his mid-nineties he still spent time shearing sheep and training others in the art of shepherding.

As I prepared my remarks for his memorial service, I began thinking about some of the major national and global crises he experienced in his ninety-five years of life. Mr. Paulson was born in the aftermath of World War I, he grew up during the Great Depression, and he lived through World War II. He experienced the Korean War and the cultural shifts of the 1950s and 60s. He experienced the Cuban Missile Crisis, the Vietnam War, the Cold War, and the massively high interest rates of the 1980s (not to mention mullet haircuts). He lived through the technological revolution, the Gulf War, 9–11, the war on terror, and the Great Recession.

Dynamic Living in Desperate Times

Amid each of these seasons of national and international conflict, Mr. Paulson maintained a consistent faith in God's overarching purposes in the world, and as I reflected on his life, a couple of things stood out to me.

First, there have always been desperate times in our world. By the time you and I die, we, too, will have a story like Don Paulson's; we will have lived through wave after wave of spiritual upheaval and national and global uncertainty and unrest. Hopefully, this thought brings comfort rather than despair. Granted, it can be disconcerting to think that there will always be tough times in our world, but it is also helpful to know that human history has *always* occurred against the backdrop of such times. Indeed, it is in the context of those times that truly great lives emerge.

Second, in addition to possessing a general acceptance of the difficulties that accompany the human narrative, we must be astute enough to understand the challenges that are unique to our specific times. In 1 Chronicles 12:32, the Scripture commends the sons of Issachar as "men who understood the times and knew what Israel should do." Just as Jeremiah had to learn to run with the horses and live a towering life amid the unique religious and social contexts of his day, so must we, and the current state of religious life in North America can best be described as increasingly post-Christian. The emergence of post-Christendom in America has radically changed the religious landscape of our Western world.

Post-Christendom

In his book, *Post-Christendom: Church and Mission in a Strange New World*, Stuart Murray defines post-Christendom as "the culture that emerges as the Christian faith loses coherence within a society that has been definitely shaped by the Christian story and as the institutions that have been developed to express Christian convictions decline in influence."[1] Post-Christian cultures are those wherein the story of Jesus is largely rejected, and the church

---

1. Murray, *Post-Christendom: Church and Mission in a Strange New World*, 9.

Your Context

cannot rely on its social, cultural, or governmental influence to sustain its existence. Post-Christendom differs from pre-Christendom in the sense that pre-Christian cultures have not been shaped by the Christian message, whereas post-Christian ones have. Post-Christian cultures are not un-churched cultures; they are Christianized cultures that have jettisoned their Christian moorings in favor of pluralism, relativity, and other spiritual pursuits.

Understandably, this shift heralds a troubling future that necessitates a response from the church. For some, the looming post-Christian horizon in America must cause us to either hope exclusively for a spiritual revival or frantically cling to our power and influence for as long as we can. Murray suggests another approach. Where some are lamenting and decrying post-Christendom, Murray sees within it an opportunity.

Although the apparent demise of Christendom in today's Western world is cause for great alarm and dismay among many Christians and church leaders, Murray sees it as a strategic opportunity for the church to rediscover its ancient, relational, Christ-oriented posture in the world. He believes that the disintegration of Christendom can actually serve the cause of Christ because it will force the church to reclaim its heritage as a counter-cultural force of service, witness, and love. Additionally, the shift from Christendom to post-Christendom will allow the church to shed some of the negative elements in its history such as its totalitarianism, religiosity, and wealth corruptions.[2] For Murray, post-Christendom and its ensuing marginalization of the Christian faith is actually the perfect breeding ground for a robust, dynamic, New Testament faith to grow.

Yes, the marginalization of the Christian church in America seems to be an inevitable effect of our increasingly post-Christian landscape, but that does not have to be an exclusively negative prospect. Christianity was birthed as a minority influence amid the iron grip of a pluralistic superpower. Today, Christianity is experiencing explosive growth in nations where it was formerly marginalized or oppressed. The death of comfortable, cultural

2. Ibid., 110.

Christianity is a far cry from the death of Christianity itself. Historically, moments like ours today have often led to positive reformation movements within the church.

Christendom began to flourish in the 300s after the Roman Emperor Constantine elevated the Christian faith to a nationally recognized and affirmed religion. Examining the church historically from Constantine to St. Augustine to the Reformation and into the twentieth century, reveals that the church has often *lost* spiritual power, witness, and effectiveness in direct correlation to the entrenchment of Christendom. Historically, Christendom would swell and spread until it brought decadence and decline, and then counter-cultural Christians would rediscover their truly biblical Christian roots and launch new movements to introduce Jesus to the world.

This is beautiful, and it is happening today. While some are lamenting the loss of the church's influence and fighting to retain its cultural and political prestige, others are desperate to more simply and accurately represent Jesus Christ in the world. These leaders are "eschewing nostalgia and welcoming the challenges and opportunities of post-Christendom."[3]

Faithful Presence

In David E. Fitch's book, *Faithful Presence: Seven Disciplines That Shape the Church for Mission*, Fitch asserts that Jesus' followers should be tangible manifestations of God's loving presence in the world. He writes, "God's plan is to become present to the world in and through a people, and then invite the world to join with Him."[4] When the church is faithfully present in our world, the world will more readily perceive that *Christ* is also present in the world. Fitch continues, "As North American Christendom wanes, with fewer and fewer Christians to be kept happy, with churches shrinking and the injustices of the world pressing on us, it has never been

---

3. Ibid., 261.

4. Fitch, *Faithful Presence: Seven Disciplines That Shape the Church for Mission*, 26.

more urgent for the church to be faithfully present in the world around us."[5]

The answer for postmodern, post-Christian cultures is not a fear-based clinging to power or a mere polemic deconstructionism that pokes holes in the culture's ways of thinking. Rather, it is a robust, hope-filled message rooted solidly in Jesus' message of the Kingdom of God. As author and pastor Todd Hunter has stated, "The Kingdom of God is a secular reality that stays close to broken humanity."[6] The Kingdom of God is a secular reality in that it is God's domain reaching out to broken humanity in all of its expressions and abodes. Despite the radical progression of scientific and technological advancements in today's world, people are still fractured and hurting, and today's post-Christian Christ-followers are called to serve as priests of God as He stands in solidarity with His broken creation, patiently drawing them back to their original purpose and function for life. In a postmodern, post-Christian world, this is our way forward.

Back to You

In addition to the external, cultural context of your specific moment in history, your personal story, with all of its highs, lows, victories, and defeats, creates a context as well. It is within the synthesis of these contexts that our lives get lived. Some people allow the pain and struggle of their context to shrink the scope and impact of their lives, while others, like Jeremiah, learn to live even more powerfully. Here is what it looks like when they do.

Dynamic lives:

1. Run in a faster heat.
2. Are fueled and sustained by a word from God.

---

5. Ibid., 30.
6. Hunter, Todd. "Church Renewal." Lecture, Azusa Pacific University Doctor of Ministry program, Azusa, CA, January 16, 2017.

3. Stretch back farther than their family of origin and connect to the "before" of God.
4. Are quick to *shuwb*/return.
5. Carry a prophetic word from the Lord for others.
6. Are carriers of hope and proclaimers of judgment—they remind people that spring is coming, and they constantly call people back to their place in God.
7. Walk the ancient path in company with Jesus Christ.
8. Rest beneath the shadow of the dread champion.
9. Respond to the master potter's touch—and only pull people *up*.
10. Let others help them when they need it.
11. Have a fire in their bones.
12. Understand their context.

"The Glory of God Is Man Fully Alive." —St. Irenaeus

It is a pretty robust list. It is inspiring and a little bit daunting, too. It encapsulates the character of Jeremiah, and it explains why people saw Jesus and immediately thought of the Old Testament prophet. Let's keep company with Jesus and Jeremiah. Let's walk with them on an ancient path where hope is born and our hearts come fully alive. Let's stand tall in our shaky, desperate times. And let's be steadfast carriers of God's light, hope, and love for our world and those who follow us. This is dynamic living.

Questions for Discussion

- What national/international crises have you already lived through in your life?
- What personal crises have you lived through?

Your Context

- How do you perceive post-Christendom and other social factors affecting our modern world?
- In light of your context how should you now live?
- What would it look like for you to be fully alive?

Bibliography

Barrett, William. *Irrational Man*. Garden City: Doubleday Anchor, 1962.
Barry, William A. *Finding God in All Things: A Companion to the Spiritual Exercises of St. Ignatius*. Notre Dame: Ave Maria, 1991.
Beeke, Joel R., and Randall J. Pederson. *Meet the Puritans: With a Guide to Modern Reprints*. Grand Rapids: Reformation Heritage, 2007.
Bennet, Arthur, ed. *The Valley of Vision: A Collection of Puritan Prayers & Devotions*. Scotland: The Banner of Truth Trust, 1975.
Bolduc, Kathleen Deyer. *The Spiritual Art of Raising Children with Disabilities*. Valley Forge: Judson, 2014.
Boyd, Gregory A. *Cross Vision: How the Crucifixion of Jesus Makes Sense of Old Testament Violence*. Minneapolis: Fortress, 2017.
Bright, John. *A History of Israel*. Philadelphia: Westminster Press, 1959.
Bright, John. *Jeremiah (Anchor Bible Series, Vol. 21)*. NY: Doubleday Religious, 1964.
Bright, John. *The Kingdom of God*. Nashville: Abingdon, 1953.
Brooks, Cleanth. *The Hidden God*. New Haven: Yale University Press, 1963.
Brother Lawrence. *The Practice of the Presence of God*. Grand Rapids: Spire, 1958, 1967.
Brown, F., S. Driver, and C. Briggs. *The Brown-Driver-Briggs Hebrew and English Lexicon*, Unabridged, Electronic Database. 2002, 2003, 2006 by Biblesoft, Inc.
Brueggemann, Walter. *A Commentary on Jeremiah: Exile and Homecoming*. Grand Rapids: William Eerdmans, 1998.
Brueggemann, Walter. *The Prophetic Imagination*. Minneapolis: Fortress, 2001.
Calhoun, Adele Ahlberg. *Spiritual Disciplines Handbook: Practices That Transform Us*. Carol Stream: InterVarsity, 2015.
Carson, Clayborne. *A Knock at Midnight*. New York: Warner, 1998.
Chesterton, G.K. *Heretics*. London: Bodley Head, 1905.
Cichetti, Dante, and Marjorie Beeghly, eds. *The Self in Transition: Infancy to Childhood*. Chicago: The University of Chicago Press, 1990.
Dempsey, Carol. *Preacher of Grace, Poet of Truth*. Collegeville: Liturgical, 2007.

Bibliography

Desmond, William. *Being and the Between: Political Theory in the American Academy.* Albany: SUNY, 1995.
De Waal, Esther. *Seeking God: The Way of St. Benedict.* Collegeville: The Liturgical, 2001.
Didapper, P.J. "Standing on the shoulders of giants," *The Pharmaceutical Journal,* 2011.
Eldredge, John. *Epic: The Story God is Telling.* Nashville: Thomas Nelson, 2004.
Elwell, Walter A. ed. *Baker's Evangelical Dictionary of Biblical Theology.* Grand Rapids: Baker, 1996.
Erickson, Millard J. *Christian Theology.* Grand Rapids: Baker Academic, 1998.
Ever After. Film. Directed by Andy Tennant. Los Angeles: Twentieth Century Fox, 1998.
Fee, Gordon D. *Paul, the Spirit, and the People of God.* Peabody: Hendrickson, Inc., 1996.
Fershleiser, Rachel, and Larry Smith, eds. *Not Quite What I Was Planning: Six-Word Memoirs by Writers Famous and Obscure.* New York: Harper Perennial, 2006.
Fitch, David E. *Faithful Presence: Seven Disciplines That Shape the Church for Mission.* Downers Grove: InterVarsity, 2016.
Fitch, David E. *The Great Giveaway.* Grand Rapids: Baker, 2005.
Freedom Writers. Film. Directed by Richard LaGravanese. Los Angeles: MTV Films and Jersey Films, 2007.
Fretheim, Terence E. *Smyth & Helwys Bible Commentary: Jeremiah.* Macon: Smyth & Helwys, 2002.
Friedman, Edwin H. *A Failure of Nerve.* New York: Seabury, 2007.
Foster, Richard. *The Celebration of Discipline: The Path to Spiritual Growth.* San Francisco: HarperCollins, 1998.
Foxe, John. *Foxe's Book of Martyrs.* Uhrichsville: Barbour, 2001.
Geisinger, Bill. "Basic Throwing." http://ceramicsweb.org 2018.
Grenz, Stanley J. *A Primer on Post-Modernism.* Grand Rapids: Eerdmanns, 1996.
Guyon, Jeanne. *Experiencing the Depths of Jesus Christ.* Beaumont: Seed Sowers, 1975.
Halley, H. H. *Halley's Bible Handbook.* Grand Rapids: Zondervan, 1965.
Harrelson, Walter J. *Jeremiah: Prophet to the Nations.* Valley Forge: Judson, 1959.
Harrison, R.K. *Jeremiah and Lamentations: An Introduction and Commentary.* Downers Grove: Inter-Varsity, 1973.
Helminiak, Daniel A. *The Human Core of Spirituality: Mind as Psyche and Spirit.* New York: Albany State University of New York Press, 1996.
Hendriksen, William. *New Testament Commentary: Galatians, Ephesians, Philippians, Colossians, and Philemon.* Grand Rapids: Baker, 1967.
Heschel, Abraham. *God in Search of Man.* New York: Farrar, Straus, and Giroux, 1955.

BIBLIOGRAPHY

Holladay, William L. *Jeremiah: A Commentary on the Book of the Prophet Jeremiah (Chapters 1–25)*. Minneapolis: Fortress, 1986.

Holladay, William L. *Jeremiah 2: A Commentary on the Book of the Prophet Jeremiah (Chapters 26–52)*. Minneapolis: Fortress, 1990.

Holladay, William L. *Jeremiah: Reading the Prophet in His Time and Ours*. Minneapolis: Fortress, 2006.

Hunter, James Davison. *To Change the World: The Irony, Tragedy, and Possibility of Christianity in the Late Modern World*. New York: Oxford University Press, 2010.

Johnson, Jan. *When the Soul Listens*. Colorado Springs: NavPress, 1999.

Keller, Phillip. *A Shepherd Looks at Psalm 23*. New York: Harper Paperbacks, 1970.

King, Jr., Martin Luther. *Strength to Love*. Philadelphia: Fortress, 1963.

Lamott, Anne. *Traveling Mercies: Some Thoughts on Faith*. New York: Random, 1992.

Lau, Benyamin. *Jeremiah: The Fate of a Prophet*. New Milford: Maggid, 2013.

London, Jack. *The Call of the Wild*. Mineola: Dover, 1990.

Lundbom, Jack R. *Jeremiah: Prophet Like Moses*. Eugene: Cascade, 2015.

Lyons, Gabe. *The Next Christians: The Good News About the End of Christian America*. New York: Doubleday Religion, 2010.

Lyotard, Jean Francois. Trans. G. Bennington and B. Massumi. *The Postmodern Condition: A Report on Knowledge*. Manchester: Manchester University Press, 1986.

Maas, Robin, and Gabriel O'Donnell. *Spiritual Traditions for the Contemporary Church*. Nashville: Abingdon, 1990.

Markey, John J. *Moses in Pharaoh's House*. Winona: Anselm Academic, 2014.

Marsh, F.E. *The Structural Principles of the Bible*. John Ritchie Ltd., 2008.

Marzano, C., Ferrara, M., Curcio, G., & Gennaro, L. "The effects of sleep deprivation in humans: Topographical electroencephalogram changes in non-rapid eye movement (NREM) sleep versus REM sleep." *Journal of Sleep Research*, 2010. https://www.ncbi.nlm.nih.gov/pubmed/19845849.

McKenzie, Steven L. "Forthtelling, Not Foretelling," *Oxford Scholarship Online*, 2018. http://www.oxfordscholarship.com/view/10.1093/acprof:o so/9780195161496.001.0001/acprof-9780195161496-chapter-3.

McLaren, Brian D. *A New Kind of Christian*. San Francisco: Jossey-Bass, 2011.

McNamara, William. *The Human Adventure*. Garden City: Image, 1976.

Meyer, F.B. *The Secret of Guidance*. Chicago: Moody, 1997, 2010.

Moo, Douglas J. and D. A. Carson. *An Introduction to the New Testament*. Grand Rapids: Zondervan, 1992.

Muggeridge, Malcolm. *A Twentieth Century Testimony*. Nashville: Thomas Nelson, 1978.

Mulholland Jr., Robert M. *Shaped by the Word: The Power of Scripture in Spiritual Formation*. Nashville: Upper Room, 2000.

Murray, Stuart. *Post-Christendom: Church and Mission in a Strange New World*. Milton Keynes: Paternoster, 2004.

BIBLIOGRAPHY

O'Connor, Kathleen M. *Jeremiah: Pain and Promise*. Minneapolis: Fortress, 2011.

Oslon, Roger E. *Reformed and Always Reforming: The Postconservative Approach to Evangelical Theology*. Grand Rapids: Baker Academic, 2007.

Peterson, Eugene. *Run with The Horses: The Quest for Life at Its Best*. Downers Grove: IVP, 2009.

Saad, Lydia. "American's Faith in Honesty, Ethics of Police Rebounds." https://news.gallup.com/poll/187874/americans-faith-honesty-ethics-police-rebounds.aspx.

Sanders, Oswald J. *Spiritual Leadership: Principles of Excellence for Every Believer*. Chicago: Moody, 1967.

Shaw, Haydn. *Generational IQ: Christianity Isn't Dying; Millennials Aren't the Problem; and the Future Is Bright*. Carol Stream: Tyndale House, 2015.

Slagle, Charles. *From the Father's Heart: A Glimpse of God's Nature and Ways*. Shippensburg: Destiny Image, 1989.

Smith, James K. A. *You Are What You Love: The Spiritual Power of Habit*. Grand Rapids: Brazos, 2016.

Stott, John R. W. *Baptism & Fullness: The Work of the Holy Spirit Today*. Downers Grove: InterVarsity, Second Edition, 1975.

Strawn, Brent A. *The Old Testament is Dying (Theological Explorations for the Church Catholic): A Diagnosis and Recommended Treatment*. Grand Rapids: Baker Academic, 2017.

Strong, James. *The New Strong's Exhaustive Concordance of the Bible*. Nashville: Thomas Nelson, 1990.

Sukel, Kayt. "Sleep Deprivation Increases Susceptibility to False Memories." http://www.dana.org/News/Sleep_Deprivation_Increases_Susceptibility_to_False_Memories/Dana.org.

The Jerusalem Bible Reader's Edition. Garden City: Doubleday & Company, Inc., 1968.

They Live. DVD. Directed by John Carpenter. Los Angeles: Alive Films and Larry Franco Productions, 1988.

Thomas a Kempis. *The Imitation of Christ*. New York: Sheed and Ward, 1959.

Thomas, Merton. *The New Man*. New York: Mentor-Omega, 1961.

Thompson, John A. *The Book of Jeremiah (New International Commentary on the Old Testament)*. Grand Rapids: William B. Eerdmans, 1980.

Willard, Dallas. *Hearing God: Developing a Conversational Relationship with God*. Madison: InterVarsity, 2012.

Willard, Dallas. *Spirit of the Disciplines: Understanding How God Changes Lives*. San Francisco: HarperCollins, 1988.

Willard, Dallas. *The Great Omission*. San Francisco: Harper One, 2006.

Wright, Christopher J. H. *The Message of Jeremiah: Against Wind and Tide*. Downers Grove: IVP Academic, 2014.

Wright, John W. *Telling God's Story: Narrative Preaching for Christian Formation*. Downers Grove: InterVarsity, 2007.

BIBLIOGRAPHY

Zodhiates, Spiros. *The Complete Word Study Dictionary New Testament.* Chattanooga: AMG, 1992.

Zodhiates, Spiros. *The Complete Word Study New Testament.* Chattanooga: AMG, 1992.

Zodhiates, Spiros. *The Complete Word Study Old Testament.* Chattanooga: AMG, 1992.

www.ingramcontent.com/pod-product-compliance
Lightning Source LLC
Chambersburg PA
CBHW050833160426
43192CB00010B/2008